Praise for *All I Need to Know I'm* Still Learning at 80

Uncommon common sense – Ronald Higdon has scored again in *All I Need to Know I'm Still Learning at 80*. Dr. Higdon has written a sagacious signpost for both the academic and the unacademic and both the young and not so young. He has given second testimony to my late father's wise council: learn something new (and I might add useful) every day of your life.

– John A. Lloyd, M.D.
Pulmonologist, Louisville, KY

There was a time in the not too distant past when some "experts" felt that adults after 30 could not learn anything new. Ron Higdon adds fuel to the fire burning for some years now that decidedly consumes that theory and reveals it as dross. This book holds special interest for life-long learners because it comes out of Higdon's many years of search for meaningful truth. As a Christian minister, he has remembered that his leader pronounced that when we know the truth, we shall be set free.

– Bob Ivan Johnson Ph.D.
Minister at Large, Consultant and Coach

With a tip of the hat to Robert Fulgham about the wisdom of the kindergarten sandpile, Ronald Higdon reminds us that learning is a life-long process. Ronald Higdon acknowledges the truth of Robert Fulgham's work, *All I Really Need to Know I Learned in Kindergarten* and puts a different spin on mental discernment. With wit and wisdom, Higdon reminds us of the possibilities that come with age, application and life-long discoveries.

The old saying, "you can't teach an old dog new tricks" does not apply to Ronald Higdon. He doesn't accept the "proverb" for himself (or for any human) and continues to grow and learn and explore—even in his eighties. Ronald Higdon is my role model and inspiration—he's an avid reader, a clear-minded thinker, and a zealous writer. Every page of this book provides fresh insights gleaned from a long life of reading, thinking, and writing.

– John Lepper
Coordinator, Retired,
Cooperative Baptist Fellowship, Kentucky

In his delightfully written book, *All I Need to Know I'm Still Learning at 80: Things I'm Still Working On*, Ron Higdon states that he wants "to leave life in the middle of a sentence." This is his witty yet profound way of saying that he recognizes that none of us should think he or she has arrived "full grown" in any arena of one's life. We are all in the process of becoming. Higdon challenges the reader to go on a journey with him through life that acknowledges the mystery, change, endings and beginnings, our humanity, grace, and the Easter reality of more to come after death. Drawing from the pool of his sixty years of pastoral experience, and from theologians, writers, humorists and others, Higdon provides in this book a life-pattern, not only for the elderly but more appropriately for those in the early stage of life's pilgrimage. His personal reflections and thoughtful questions at the end of each chapter offer time for one to examine his or her response to the writer's challenge. Joining Higdon in his continuing learning experience will enliven and enrich anyone who will take the journey through this commanding book.

– William Powell Tuck
Retired Pastor and Seminary Professor
Author of *Star Thrower: A Pastor's Handbook* and *Holidays, Holy Days and Special Days.*

All I Need to Know
I'm Still Learning at 80
Things I'm Still Working On

Ronald Higdon

[signature: Ron Higdon]

Energion Publications
Gonzalez, FL
2017

ISBN10: 1-63199-384-4
ISBN13: 978-1-63199-384-8
Library of Congress Control Number: 2017940055

Energion Publications
P. O. Box 841
Gonzalez, FL 32560
850-525-3916

energion.com
pubs@energion.com

DEDICATION

This book is dedicated to one of the best friends I ever had: Perry Bramlett. His untimely death in 2013 left a hole in my life that will never be filled. He introduced me to more writers and authors than I could have ever found on my own. Our almost weekly trips to used bookstores resulted in "finds" that were mind and life changing. Perry's writings and knowledge of C. S. Lewis were respected in the highest academic circles. He was the only person in the United States who taught and wrote about Lewis as a full-time vocation. I invited him to do a "Weekend with C.S. Lewis" in almost every one of my interims. The response of the congregation was always the same: "We've got to have Perry back." His unmatched collection of C. S. Lewis writings and memorabilia is now housed in a special room in the library at Mercer University. It is to his memory and with deep gratitude that I dedicate this book.

ACKNOWLEDGMENTS

The Bibliography lists those books from which I have quoted. There are many and I am grateful for the major part that reading has played in my continuing education. But that is certainly not the whole story. Another crucial ingredient has been the relationships that have enriched my life, taught me much, and challenged me in ways that caring people do. The first "thank you" goes to my wife, Pat, and my sons Michael and my late son, Mark. Those who know me best have had the love and patience to hang in there with me in the times that it didn't seem as though I had learned very much. I could not have made it to this point without their affirmation and support.

Like an acceptance speech at the Academy Awards, to thank all the people in my life who deserve words of appreciation would be endless: the many friends, the teachers in college, seminary, graduate studies and those whose lectures and workshops I attended through the years brought new insights and often pointed me in new directions, plus the many congregations I served through my over sixty years of ministry that provided the greatest "on-site" workshops in faith and living I could ever have hoped for.

I, indeed, owe so much to so many.

TABLE OF CONTENTS

INTRODUCTION

Blessed are those whose strength is in you,
whose hearts are set on pilgrimage. – Psalm 84:5

My current plan is to leave this life in the middle of a sentence and enter a time and place where, I not only complete that sentence, but begin another one that is part of an entirely new chapter. In *Finnegans Wake*, James Joyce ends the story in mid-sentence without punctuation or explanation. This reference comes from Robert Fulghum's fifteenth anniversary revision of his classic *All I Really Need to Know I Learned In Kindergarten*.

Fulghum never intended the title to be taken literally but simply attempted to list what he terms some elemental pieces of wisdom that came very early in life. "Wisdom was not at the top of the graduate-school mountain, but there in the sandpile at Sunday School."[1] He asks his readers to take the items he lists and extrapolate them into sophisticated adult terms in order to apply them to all areas in our lives. His book then gives story-essays, really parables, that provide the starting point for reflection and conversation.

I believe Fulghum would agree that "still learning" continues to come at eighty. At sixty-five (his age in 2003 when he penned his revision) he writes:

> I have reconsidered, revised, and expanded this book as part of a cycle of rethinking about where I've been, where I am, and where I'm going. If all goes well, I will keep on doing that, and come back to Kindergarten again and[2]

In the Joyce tradition, he ends his revision in the middle of a sentence with no punctuation. He does, however, provide some prior explanation. This book will not literally end in the middle

---

1   Robert Fulghum, *All I Really Need to Know I Learned in Kindergarten*,
     15th Anniversary Edition (New York: Ballantine Books, 2003), 2.
2   Ibid, 219.

of a sentence but with the implied "to be continued" clearly understood.

Not being a great fan of tee-shirt slogans, I have nonetheless been on the lookout for one I would not be able to resist wearing. "Under Construction" would carry the message that speaks to the incompleteness of just about everything. Another choice of my own design would be: "On the Road Again," changed to read: "On the Road Always." This, of course, speaks to the traditional concept of the Christian life as pilgrimage which is well-documented in Scripture and in the writings of Bunyan and countless others. Paul says it this way: ... *not ... that I have reached my goal, but I am still pursuing it....* (Philippians 3:12: NJB).

A modern expression of that idea comes from the NBC Today Show of March 8, 1995, when Bryan Gumbel asked Maya Angelou what was on her "Wish List." With all that she has accomplished in her life, could there be any more objectives, any more conditions unfulfilled? Her response:

> "On, my Lord, yes," she exclaimed. "I want to become a better writer. I'm very serious about it. It's what I am. It's how I describe myself to myself, and I want to be a better human being. I'm trying to be a Christian, which is no small matter. I mean it – I'm always amazed…when people walk up to me and say, 'I'm a Christian.' I always think, 'Already? You've already got it? My goodness.'"[3]

Thomas Merton speaks to the undergirding thesis of this book: "We do not want to be beginners. But let us be convinced of the fact that we will never be anything else but beginners, all our life!"[4] Merton's essay "Learning to Live" was written in 1967 for a proposed volume on Columbia University's alumni. It was

---

3 *Homiletics Journal*, November 1997, 36.
4 Thomas Merton, *Contemplative Prayer* (New York: Image Books, 1969), 30.

first published after Merton's death. The draft copy has the title "Learning to Learn."[5]

This "learning to learn" is one of the reasons life has such an "unfinished" feel about it – even at age eighty. I have just begun to understand so many things that will definitely reshape and redirect my life. Every day brings new discoveries of beginning again. An ancient adage I read long ago suggests that there are seventy ways of reading the Bible, one for each year of one's life. I keep revising that number because I continue making discoveries not only in Scripture but in other books that now speak in new and amazing ways. I want to ask, "Why didn't I see this sooner?"

In this book you will read some of the things I have discovered so far in my journey of exploration. I have given fourteen of what I would also term essentials that are not meant to be exhaustive but representative. Questions are found at the end of each chapter for reflection and discussion. Just as there is always more to any story (Fulgham has a great chapter on this), likewise there is always an "but on the other hand." That is why learning continues and is always enhanced by community. I invite you to join me in working on some things I have found to be of paramount importance in my continuing education.

5   Lawrence S. Cunningham, *Thomas Merton: Spiritual Master* (New York: Paulist Press, 1992), 357f.

Chapter 1

There Are No Trains To Yesterday

If you, Lord, kept a record of sins,
Lord, who could stand? – Psalm 130:3

Waiting at the Depot

Eric Weiner poses a question for which the answer is not as obvious as it might first seem: "Is there any moment other than the present?"[6] After the death of our older, bipolar son to suicide in 2013, my wife and I found ourselves in line with countless others at the Regret station waiting for the "If Only" express.

If there had been a train to yesterday we would gladly have boarded it in order to do all those things we believed might have prevented our terrible loss. We relived what we thought in hindsight were moments of opportunity to change the outcome of this horrible condition. We read numerous books that listed the three most common emotions associated with this kind of loss: shame, guilt, and anger. We experienced all of them but guilt overrode the other two.

Logically, we knew there was no Wellsian time machine to transport us to the past. But this was one of those times when rationality took a back seat to the emotions that were driving our lives. It was too painful to dwell in the present moment so we kept thinking about "What if?"

---

6   Eric Weiner, *Man Seeks God* (New York: Twelve, 2011), 216.

All of this is a part of the grief journey that one must take if there is ever going to be any possibility of moving ahead. I wrote *Surviving a Son's Suicide*[7] as a part of that journey and also to bear witness that it is possible finally to begin inching one's foot out the door into reinvestment in life. The three emotions associated with suicide continue to wait in the wings ready to make a brief appearance but, thankfully, they no longer have center stage.

As one gets older, it is an increasing challenge to refuse the gift that keeps on giving: guilt. That idea is one of the many words of wisdom from the late Erma Bombeck that I found in a book of *Quirky Quotations*.[8] Unfortunately, it is not all that quirky but is a driving emotion in the lives of so many disappointed and disillusioned people. After a reasonable amount of time (which varies greatly according to a multitude of factors), one has to begin to counter guilt's assault with: "All things considered, under all the circumstances, I did the best I knew how."

PUTTING THINGS IN THE TRASH BIN

Hopefully, we finally reach the point where we are able to heed some of the best advice I have ever read: "If you want God's fire to burn brightly in your heart, take out yesterday's ashes."[9] In an early pastorate, I was visited by a man who came to see me about what he termed his "problem." It was our first meeting and he looked a little disheveled. I had already heard that he was the kind and gentle neighborhood alcoholic. He wanted me to do something for him. He asked if I would talk to his wife who had left him. Something he said raised a question in my mind and I asked, "How long has she been gone?" He replied, "Fifteen years!" I said very calmly, "I think she's probably decided to stay gone."

---

7   Ronald Higdon, *Surviving a Son's Suicide* (Gonzalez, FL: Energion Publications, 2014).

8   Tad Tuleja, *Quirky Quotations* (New York: Galahad Books, 1992), 106.

9   Joseph Roberts, Jr., *Sideswiped by Eternity* (Louisville: John Knox Press, 2006), 115.

In sharp contrast to that story is one I read from the life of Shirley Temple. At seven, she was the most popular movie star in the world. When she retired from the movies at twenty-two, she had earned over three million dollars. Her father had quit his job to oversee her finances. Through the years he not only failed to make the payments into a court-ordered trust fund, but had spent all but $44,000 of her fortune. Her friends urged her to sue but she told them: "My attitude has always been to get it over with and get on with it." She even took care of her father during his final illness.[10]

Refusing to keep focused on yesterday is always a decision. For me, it continues to be an ongoing fragmental decision – various pieces at a time. Looking back over almost sixty years of pastoral and interim ministries, I continue to deal with those moments when I did not bring the best wisdom to situations. Often, it was wisdom that I did not have at that moment. Being patient with who I was and where I was in a specific time and place is an ongoing achievement. Nothing is ever going to undo what I wish I had done another way. There is no way to unravel the twisted threads of a long ago situation. I'm trying to abide by the advice that is tough but needed: "I knew a very wise woman once. When anyone started in on the subject of what might have been she always cut them off with, 'What might have been, wasn't; get on with your life.'"[11]

NOSTALGIA IS NOT WHAT IT USED TO BE

The "Regret" station is not the only one where people are waiting to board. The other is "Nostalgia" where people strain to see the "Glory Days" limited coming into view. In times of high anxiety (and when have there ever been any other times?), it is always a temptation to dwell on treasured memories of another era.

I immediately think of the supposed response of Horace Greeley to the charge that his newspaper was not as good as it used to

---

10 Geoffrey C. Ward, *American Originals* (New York: HarperCollins, 1991), 59.

11 Robert Farrar Capon, *The Mystery of Christ & Why We Don't Get It* (Grand Rapids: Eerdmans, 1993), 112.

be: "It never was." As the future gets darker and darker, the past often gets better and better. Our memories have great filtering and reshaping systems that call for frequent reality checks.

Somewhere I picked up the story of a Bishop who was meeting with a group of local pastors. He announced he had good news and bad news and asked which they would like first. "Give us the bad news!" So the Bishop said, "It is now more difficult than ever to be in pastoral ministry." Most simply nodded in agreement and then asked for the good news. The Bishop smiled and announced, "If the fifties ever come back, we're ready!"

Doing church in the twenty-first century is totally different from anything most of us were trained for in seminary. Our "church world" is gone. The church does not dominate the culture and we live in a pluralistic society and a global world. We are truly in a time of transition; we are at one of the hinge points in history. Nothing is ever going to bring back a time that is no more.

THE HERE AND NOW

I found this poem in one of my files and believe it is a good summary to this chapter. It comes from the pen of Helen Mallicoat:

> I was regretting the past
> and fearing the future.
> Suddenly my Lord was speaking:
> "My name is I AM." He paused.
> I waited. He continued.
> "When you live in the past,
> with its mistakes and regrets,
> it is hard. I am not there.
> My name is not I Was.
> When you live in the future,
> with its problems and its fears,
> it is hard. I am not there.
> My name is not I Will Be.

When you live in this moment,
it is not hard. I am here.
My name is I Am."

My only disagreement with the philosophy expressed is that often living in the present moment is hard. What makes it so difficult is implied in the oft-quoted words of Irenaeus: "The glory of God is a human being fully alive." If I live with heavy emotional investments in the past and the future, do I have enough left over to be fully alive in the now? My personal confessional answer: no. Too often in my life I was like the fictional character who leaped on his horse and rode off in all four directions. But as the title of this book indicates, I'm continuing to work on this. I am making progress and this for me is the acid test.

A famous rabbi passed away and one of his disciples was being interviewed. In exploring the reasons for the rabbi's fame, the reporter asked: "What was most important in the life of your teacher?" "Whatever he happened to be doing at the moment," came the quick reply. I interpret this to mean being fully present in the moment. The power of a fully-present person is known only by those who have been blessed with this all too rare experience.

In this age of distraction, it is incredibly difficult for people to observe what has been termed "the sacrament of the present moment" or "the sacredness of the present moment." It involves giving another the greatest gift we have to offer – the gift of ourselves in full attention mode. For a culture of multi-tasking and constant-connections, this seems almost an impossible mode to enter. My suggestion is to begin with brief segments of time: ten minutes of undivided focus as you sit with a family member or friend. Then brief periods of time during the day as you encounter people in your ordinary routine.

In my choices of times in which to live, is there really any other option than the present? Is there any other way to do this except to be fully present?

AFTERTHOUGHT

James Thurber: "Let us not look back in anger or forward in fear, but around in awareness."[12]

PERSONAL REFLECTIONS

In the eighth decade of my life, I'm still working on:

- How to spend less time poring over the records of past failures and regrets.
- Making it a daily task to spend less time grieving over what will never be as it once was.
- Trying to get rid of the "dead" things in my life in order to make room for things that are alive and well.
- Beginning each day with the determination to be fully alive in the present.

QUESTIONS FOR REFLECTION AND DISCUSSION

1. Have you discovered any strategies or rituals that help you forgive yourself and stop dwelling on ways in which you know you missed the mark in the past?
2. When you hear "If I had my life to live over," what are the things that immediately come to mind?
3. If you were going to carry out yesterday's ashes, what would be in that bucket?
4. What do you consider the "glory days" of your life? Why?
5. What are the things that are keeping you from being fully alive in the present?

---

12 Marcus Braybrooke, *Life Lines* (New York: Thorsons, 2002), 53.

Chapter 2

Change: One Thing I Can Count On

I have seen something else under the sun:
The race is not to the swift,
or the battle to the strong,
nor does food come to the wise
or wealth to the brilliant
or favor to the learned;
but time and chance happen to them all. – Ecclesiastes 9:11

"Those Were the Days: We Thought They'd Never End"

A popular song of bygone days (where most of my favorite songs are to be found) summarizes how most of us experience the earlier part of our lives. We simply can't imagine things being other than what they are and as they are. When I tell you that the world in which I have lived most of my life is no more, you understand that. My dad used to brag that he had lived in a time of amazing progress: he saw his first automobile when he was a small boy and lived to see a man walk on the moon. The world of that first automobile and what immediately followed is certainly no more. The space age inaugurated an entirely new age that shows no sign of slowing down.

For needed comic relief, I often turn to writers like Lewis Grizzard. In his book *Elvis Is Dead and I Don't Feel So Good Myself,* he echoes my sentiments with this line: "The everlasting dilemma facing me is that although I live in a new world, I was reared to live in the old one."[13] How else can you possibly be reared than to live in the world in which you are growing up?

When an old Kentucky farmer was asked: "I bet you've seen a lot of changes in farming in your lifetime, haven't you?" his response was, "I sure have. And I've been against every one of them!" That attitude helps create the problem of taking yesterday's prescriptions for today's ailments. Of taking the viewpoint of the past as the only way to see things. Of insisting that: "As it was in the beginning, so it is now, and so it shall ever be." Because it won't. It's the classic mistake of using heritage as a millstone instead of a stepping stone.

When did all this change begin? My answer to that question is a story that didn't make it into the Bible. As Adam and Eve are walking out of the Garden of Eden, Adam turns to Eve and laments, "My dear, we are living in changing and challenging times!" And so has it ever been. Change is the one thing you can count on. Things are not going to remain the same. "The first lesson of history, and it may be the last, is that you never know what is coming next."[14]

A TIME OF TRANSITIONALITY

The kind of time in which we live - a time of extremely rapid change, often referred to as one of the hinge points of history – is a time of high anxiety. William Bridges in a book written in 1980 was already forecasting the future: "Stuck in transition, many Americans are caught in a semipermanent condition of transitionality."[15] He describes them as "suffering the confusing nowhere of in-betweeness."[16]

---

13 Lewis Grizzard, *Elvis Is Dead and I Don't Feel So Good Myself* (Atlanta: Peachtree Publishing, 1984), 40.

14 G. M. Young, quoted in Patrick Henry, *The Ironic Christian's Companion* (New York: Riverhead Books, 1999), 170.

15 William Bridges, *Transitions: Making Sense of Life's Changes* (Reading, MA: Addison-Wesley Publishing, 1980), 4.

16 Ibid, 5.

There are so many firsts that have occurred during my lifetime that I hardly know where the list would end. Attending Saturday movie matinées as a boy watching Buck Rogers' serials hardly prepared me for a first that continues to amaze me: we are the first generation to see earth from outer space, to see the earth as a tiny ball suspended in nothing. Galileo's critics would never believe that, not only is our earth not the center of the solar system, it is not even the center of our galaxy – and our galaxy is not the center of the billions of other galaxies.

There's Always An Option

There is an old cavalry motto: "When your horse dies, dismount and saddle another."[17] Lewis Smedes cites this motto that makes you wonder, "Who would ever be dumb enough not to know this?" Our problem is that things that are just as lifeless as a deceased animal are still believed to be alive and kicking. And we don't know why we can't ride them with the same kind of good feeling and success we enjoyed in the past.

In a future chapter we will talk more about endings, but wisdom is always needed to discern what is no longer feasible or workable in the culture and world in which we now live. In serving as an intentional interim, on more occasions than I care to count, intelligent church members would call for a return to something that had brought their church excitement and growth fifty years ago. They took no thought of a much changed neighborhood, an aging congregation, completely different social and cultural tastes and priorities, and totally new forms of connection and communication.

Smedes places the old cavalry motto in the context of hope: "Hope does not have to die when hopes die. It only needs to be readjusted to fit the new reality that the death of one hope left with us. Call it 'hope adjustment' – getting old hopes in sync with new

---

17 Lewis Smedes, *Standing on the Promises* (Nashville: Thomas Nelson Publishers, 1998), 84.

reality."[18] Change always brings a new reality. We usually find this disturbing because we have learned to feel comfortable with the old reality and often have a lot of fear about what adjustment to this new reality will mean.

Ashleigh Brilliant (his real name) is the creator of what he terms "Pot Shots," bits of illustrated humorous wisdom that I frequently use in my workshops. This one is from his book, *I Have Abandoned My Search for Truth, and Am Now Looking for A Good Fantasy*: "I can no longer face life, so I've decided to go through the rest of it backwards."[19] This is always one of our options. Logically we know there isn't much present or future in such an approach. My new reality is that I am no longer forty-five. Everything in my life needs to be tailored to the reality of what life is like now that I am eighty. Trying to relive another time and place is a hopeless substitute for living fully in this time and this place.

SOUNDS SIMPLE, BUT IT'S TRUE

"Every tomorrow has two handles. We can take hold of it by the handle of anxiety or by the handle of faith."[20] These words speak to one of the basic choices I am offered every day: fear or faith. The first book I ever wrote is titled *From Fear to Faith: The Spiritual Journey from Anxiety to Trust*.[21] When I use the word "faith" I use the term in the way it is generally used in Scripture - as trust. Biblically, I see the opposite of faith not as doubt but as fear. In Mark 4:40 Jesus asks his disciples, "Why are you afraid? Have you no faith?"

Trust means that in changing times I continue to trust the One who has brought me safely thus far. I need to keep reminding myself that in the almost completely changed world in which I

18 Ibid.

19 Ashleigh Brilliant, *I Have Abandoned My Search for Truth, and Am Now Looking for a Good Fantasy* (Santa Barbara: Woodbridge Press Publishing, 1991), 84.

20 John Ed Mathison, *Treasures of the Transformed Life* (Nashville: Abingdon Press, 2006), 99.

21 Ronald Higdon, *From Fear to Faith* (Cleveland, TN: Parson's Porch Books, 2011).

find myself, God remains the same yesterday, today, and forever in his faithfulness, grace, love, mercy, and care. I keep reminding myself that peace and security are always within me and not in my circumstances which all too often give few reasons for either. The Hebrews found it just as difficult as we do to trust God on the banks of a sea and in a wilderness. In every new set of circumstances (Pharaoh's army in hot pursuit, not finding a source of water, etc.), God's people fell back into the anxiety mode because their focus was on circumstances.

Change always comes with a challenge: "Safety and security take back seats to creativity and courage."[22] In my eighth decade of life I continue to realize that, aside from the possibility of ever really achieving them, majoring on safety and security creates a very small world. Decisions based on these two requirements will certainly keep me from living a life of "radical amazement." Judy Cannato writes: "It requires gut-wrenching honesty and the willingness to give up fear-filled control" to live in "radical amazement...a culti- vated way of life filled with attentiveness and vision."[23]

AM I FINISHED?

I have found many writers saying, in various ways, that when you are through changing, you are through. New situations have brought me opportunities for growth and development. I would like to tell you that I found this to be relatively easy and quite pain- less. Probably most of the important changes (all of which came gradually) I have made in my life have come with gut-wrenching honesty and pain. I confess that I have learned too many of the things I need to know the hard way – through the experience of doing them the wrong way.

Somewhere I picked up a story of a group of frogs hopping from one side of a muddy road to a pond on the other side. One of them jumps into a deep rut and makes several unsuccessful

22 Judy Cannato, *Radical Amazement* (Notre Dame: Sorin Books, 2006), 139.
23 Ibid, 11, 14.

attempts to get out. A froggy buddy comes over and encourages him to come on with the group. "I've tried but I just can't get out. The rut is too deep." The other frogs continue on their journey and have been splashing in the pond for a short time when they see their companion hopping his way toward them. His froggy buddy inquires, "I thought you said the rut was so deep you couldn't get out?" "I did," he replied, "but this big truck came along and I had to!"

I won't bore you with all the big trucks that have come roaring down the muddy road in my life but I also found that regardless of how deep the rut I was in, I had to get out. I had to change my attitude, my stance, my belief on how something should work, the way I related to certain individuals, and generally the way I was coming at things. When I look back at the pastor I was in 1965 in my first church out of seminary, I hardly recognize that person. That is certainly not who I am now. There is certainly much to be said for long term pastorates but I have been blessed by the two student pastorates, four senior pastor situations, and the seven intentional interims I have had. Blessed because each situation was different and called upon me to slowly make significant changes. All of these positions were places of listening and learning.

All I need to know I truly am still learning at eighty. The time of changing is not over (at least my wife certainly hopes not!). New discoveries are being made because I am at a different place and I see things differently than I did before. Change forces a fresh look, a re-evaluation, and an honest appraisal of what can be done differently to deal with the new situation. The guidelines that governed my life when I was thirty are generally not appropriate for me now. They were for a different time and a different place. One basic question remains: in the new world in which I find myself, how can I live creatively, fully, and redemptively?

Afterthought

I devoted an earlier book to the subject of change: *In Changing Times: A Guide for Reflection and Conversation.*[24] Although it is one in the series sponsored by the Academy of Parish Clergy designed to provide clergy with resources written by practitioners, it speaks to the everyday world we all inhabit.

Personal Reflections

In the eighth decade of my life, I'm still working on:

- Accepting the changes that have brought about the world in which I now live.
- Making adjustments (slowly and often painfully) to the circumstances that now make up my day.
- Realizing that the most important ingredient in my life is my trust in the One who, in a changing world, remains the same in his grace, mercy, love, and care.
- Realizing that there never comes a time that I do not need fresh vision and courage to change and grow in order to live creatively and redemptively.

Questions for Reflection and Discussion

1. How has the world in which you live changed?
2. Do you feel as though we are living at one of the hinge points in history? Why or why not?
3. What are some of the things you have found most difficult to accept in your changed world?
4. Where are the areas in your life where you feel yourself most anxious and find it most difficult to exercise trust?
5. What are the some of the changes you have made in your life in response to the different world in which you now live?

---

24 Ronald Higdon, *In Changing Times* (Gonzalez, FL: Energion Publications, 2015).

Chapter 3

The Focus Is on Input, Not Outcome

Commit your way to the Lord;
trust in him and he will do this:
He will make your righteous reward shine like the dawn,
your vindication like the noonday sun.– Psalm 37:5-6

But If Not

These three words represent the most important decision any of us can ever make and it's one of those decisions that has to be renewed daily. In the third chapter of the biblical book of Daniel, three Hebrew young men are called before the Babylonian king to answer for their refusal to bow down and worship the golden image he has set up. He assures them that the consequences of their stance will result in being thrown into a furnace of blazing fire.

The writer presents this account as a contest between the gods of Babylon and Yahweh, the God of Israel. This time of exile was especially challenging because it appears on the surface that Yahweh has not been victorious in his battle against the gods of Babylon. Nebuchadnezzar's challenge to Shadrach, Meshach, and Abednego is stated in this context: *"If you do not worship, you shall immediately be thrown into a furnace of blazing fire, and who is the god that will deliver you out of my hands?"* (Daniel 3:15).

Rather than speaking to the king about their confidence in Yahweh to protect them in their faithfulness, they respond with something other than the "name it and claim it" philosophy. They do not presume on the mind and purposes of God. Their response to Nebuchadnezzar's threat is the classic commitment to input as opposed to outcome:

Shadrach, Meshach, and Abednego answered the king. "O Nebuchadnezzar, we have no need to present a defense to you in this manner. If our God whom we serve is able to deliver us from the furnace of blazing fire and out of your hand, O king, let him deliver us. BUT IF NOT, be it known to you, O king, that we will not serve your gods and we will not worship the golden statue that you have set up." (Daniel 3:16-18).

The Hebrew young men tell the king in no uncertain terms that they have already decided what they are going to do – regardless of the consequences. They are in charge of the input in this situation; they have no control over what then will happen. This is the stance based on doing what is right because it is right.

LETTING GO

Several years ago I wrote a book titled *But If Not*. Occasionally, I need to go back and read the following section to remind myself of what I continue to believe:

> What they (the Hebrew young men) tell the king is, "We know what we must do, regardless of how things turn out." The focus is where it ought to be: on actions and not on results. The first question in faith (and life) is always: "What ought I to do?" The first question is not: "What will happen to me?" This is what the art of letting go is all about; it is all about input, not about outcome. It's all about walking by faith, not by sight.[25]

The subtitle of the above book is *Mastering the Art of Letting Go*. Richard Rohr writes: "All great spirituality is somehow about letting go. Trust me on this crucial point."[26] Gandhi lived by what he termed *nishkama-kama*. This term means "actions without desire," letting go of attachment to the consequences of one's actions.[27]

---

25 Ronald Higdon, *But If Not* (Cleveland, TN: Parson's Porch Books, 2011), 21-22.

26 Richard Rohr, *The Naked Now* (New York: Crossroad Publishing, 2009), 64.

27 William H. Shannon, *Seeking the Face of God* (New York: Crossroad Publishing, 1988), 155.

This is basically a control issue. The older I get the more I become aware of how little control I have over almost everything in life. Many of my major frustrations have come from my attempts to control the uncontrollable. All such attempts should come with this warning label: "Nothing suffocates the life force more thoroughly than trying to control what is happening."[28] This quote comes from a book titled *The Second Half of Life*. Most of us finally come to believe the quote because our experiences have validated its truth.

The life force is suffocated when we major on control. Spontaneity, exploration, openness, adventuring, and a great many other things that make life worth living are put on a back shelf. This does not mean that I shouldn't carefully weigh my actions in serious situations or that I should not seek wise counsel. The final place for my decisions comes from attempting to listen to the voice of the Spirit, to that deep place within my true self, and coming to feel, "This is what I ought to do."

A Trust Issue

"The spiritual life is not about control; it's about relinquishment. It's about letting go of our need to determine and order life, and then trusting grace."[29] The trust issue is the basic issue throughout the entire Bible. Whenever God's people decide that Yahweh doesn't know best and decide to take matters into their own hands, the results are always disastrous. The psalms are filled with challenges to trust in the God who is trustworthy. Here are Jesus' words in John 14 from the King James translation: *"Do not let your hearts be troubled. Believe in God, believe also in me."* The better (and I believe more accurate) translation in contemporary Bibles is: *"Do not let your hearts be troubled. Trust in God; trust also in me."*

Belief can mean little more than intellectual ascent to a list of propositions. Trust involves placing one's life in the care of a lov-

---

28　Angeles Arrien, *The Second Half of Life* (Boulder: Sounds True, 2005), 269.

29　Chuck Queen, *The Good News According to Jesus* (Macon: Smyth & Helwys, 2009), 93.

ing God who can be counted on to lead us by his grace and never abandon us regardless of what happens. It is an ongoing confidence that we are led by a loving shepherd, even if his leadership takes us through some very dark valleys. Our trust is not determined by circumstances or by looking ahead to what might happen but by confidence in the one who is journeying through life with us.

Sometimes I have gotten the question, "How can I be sure that I am doing the right thing? Is there a sign that will let me know I'm not off course?" The answer I have given myself to this question is the only one I have to give. As Moses continues in his protests that he is not the one to confront Pharaoh, God promises him a sign:

> *But Moses said to God, "Who am I that I should go to Pharaoh, and bring the Israelites out of Egypt?" He said, "I will be with you; and this shall be the sign for you that it is I who sent you: when you have brought the people out of Egypt, you shall worship God on this mountain."* (Exodus 3:11-12).

Interpreted, this means: "God says, 'You will know that I have been with you when you have completed the mission impossible on which I am sending you.'"[30] "You will know for sure when it is over." "After the fact" doesn't seem like much of a sign but it is the only one God gives to Moses. "One thing is for sure: the will of God is much clearer in retrospect than it is in prospect."[31] It seems to be a common experience that as we look back we able to discern the hand of God in our lives in ways that were impossible to see at the time.

STARTING WITH THE SIMPLE THINGS

Most of us will never be faced with a decision like that of the three in the book of Daniel. Most of our choices are not filled with this much drama and are not nearly so public. Our playing field is much smaller and we often feel that much we do is of lit-

---

30 Patrick Henry, *The Ironic Christian*, 103.

31 Charles E. Poole, *Beyond the Broken Lights* (Macon: Smyth & Helwys, 2000), 45.

tle consequence. Our input into life frequently does require us to choose between the good and the better, between the safe and the challenging, between two things, neither of which will result in a furnace of blazing fire.

How do we know which things are important enough to weigh carefully before choosing a course of action? What about those ordinary things that make up most of our daily lives? "The spirituality that emerges from the Rule of St. Benedict is a spirituality charged with living the ordinary extraordinarily well. Here transforming life rather than transcending life is what counts."[32] Benedict calls for monastery life to be focused on the routine, the ordinary, the daily. It is not focused on becoming a super saint.

When my situation seemed insignificant and "out of the way," I was always encouraged by Mother Teresa's words: "We are not called to do great things but to do small things with great love."[33] I believe this philosophy does transform life by enabling us to live the ordinary extraordinarily well. If Brother Lawrence could wash pots and pans to the glory of God, what is to prevent my bringing this kind of commitment to everything I do? Well, it's a challenge because we often feel, "What does this matter, anyway?" But in God's world, everything matters – like a cup of cold water given in his name. In our lives everything matters, because it is these repeated daily tasks that are shaping us.

My dad did not have much formal education but he had gained much practical wisdom in his life. He repeatedly told me, "Bring your very best to whatever you have to do. When you have a paying job, always give one-hundred-ten percent. Give more than is expected." He never asked about any minimum requirements – that keeps life at a minimum. And it keeps a person feeling small. The pride and personal satisfaction that comes from bringing your best to the mundane and the ordinary are rewards enough. But when you add the Christian dimension of being a faithful servant

---

32 Joan Chittister, *Wisdom Distilled from the Daily* (New York: HarperSanFrancisco, 1990), 6.
33 Wayne Muller, *Sabbath* (New York: Bantam Books, 1999), 174.

wherever you find yourself, it brings all the little things in life to the level of a high calling.

My input, regardless of when or where, small or great, noticed or unnoticed, is extremely important. And it will always be on a higher level when I just leave the outcome to God. All the results are finally in his hands anyway so why not begin let go of what never belongs to us? With Paul I have to confess that I have not already attained my goal, but I press on!

AFTERTHOUGHT

Thomas Kelly said that this world was too vast and a lifetime too short for me to assume that I could carry all responsibilities. He said that God "does not burden us equally with all things, but considerately puts upon each of us just a few central tasks, as emphatic responsibilities." He concluded, "We cannot die on every cross, nor are we expected to."[34]

PERSONAL REFLECTIONS

In my eighth decade of life, I'm still working on:

- How to begin my decision-making with the question: "What do I believe deep down is the right thing to do?"
- To let go of the things I really know are beyond my control.
- To begin majoring on my best input into the ordinary, everyday things of life.
- To accept that many times I won't know for certain that I have made the right decision until everything is over.

QUESTIONS FOR REFLECTION

1. Are there decisions and commitments in your life you have already made before a given situation calls for them?

---

34 William P. Clemmons, *Discovering the Depths* (Victoria, BC: Tafford Publishing, 2006), 90.

2. What are the things in your life you find most difficult to let go of attempts to control?

3. What do you think about God's sign to Moses that God had really sent him to bring his people out of Egypt?

4. What examples of "washing pots and pans for the glory of God" do you find the most difficult to put into practice?

5. In what ways do you attempt to bring your very best into everything you do?

Chapter 4

It's All About Endings and Beginnings

Those who sow with tears
will reap with joy.
Those who go out weeping
carrying seed to sow
will return with songs of joy,
carrying sheaves with them. – Psalm 126: 5-6

It Is Inevitable

Every hello that has ever been spoken has had a goodbye tucked away somewhere deep inside, waiting for some moving day or some graduation day or some retiring or relocating or dying day, some eventual, inevitable someday when the goodbye that was hidden in the hello will find its way out into the open.[35]

As we age, those goodbyes find their way out into the open with a frequency that is alarming if we don't have the context of faith in which to hear them. In the chapter about change we talked about the inevitable things in life that keep bringing us into a new time and place. In this chapter, we are talking about things over which we are required to write: "finished," "no more," "the end." This is never an easy task but, unless we learn how to man-

---

35 Charles E. Poole, *The Tug of Home* (Macon: Peake Road, 1997), 79.

age endings well, we will have great difficulty executing successful beginnings.

I bought the book for the title and found it filled with stories that both inspire and challenge. The book is *Will Jesus Buy Me a Double-Wide: 'Cause I Need More Room For My Plasma TV*; the author is Karen Spears Zacharias. This brief scene is from the book:

> "I'm sorry," she said, apologizing for her tears.
> "Don't be," I replied. "If these things aren't worth crying over, what is?"[36]

Moving from an ending to a new beginning always involves the recognition of loss and taking time to fully grieve that loss. The space between an ending and a new beginning depends on how significant it is in our lives. When we lost our older son in 2013, my wife and I had difficulty realizing that he was gone. We kept expecting the phone to ring with one of his almost daily calls or for him to walk through the door for one of his holiday visits. It was not so much a denial as it was the emotional inability to deal all at once with such a devastating loss. It was certainly something worth crying over – it was not an option. My book *Surviving a Son's Suicide* describes ways that helped us make the continuing journey through grief. It was the most challenging goodbye we have ever faced.

HOW LONG DOES IT TAKE?

How long it takes to wrap-up an ending depends on many things – including our emotional makeup and the personal history of how we have handled endings in the past. In one sense, some endings will never be complete and are never meant to be. We will never forget that our son lived and the blessing he was in our lives. The kind of new beginning that is required in the loss of persons we love is about structuring life without the presence of that indi-

---

36 Karen Spears Zacharias, *Will Jesus Buy Me a Double-Wide: 'Cause I Need More Room for my Plasma TV* (Grand Rapids: Zondervan, 2010), 34.

vidual. It does not mean forgetting them; it means building a life in which they no longer have a part. This is not done quickly or all at once. We are still working on it three years later.

Some endings we postpone by our own inability to deal with the emotions that surround them. The classic story about Yogi Berra is a case in point. He played catcher for ten World Series championships with the New York Yankees. Later, in 1985, after serving a stint as manager, he was fired by owner George Steinbrenner - this after only sixteen games into the season. He vowed he would never return to the stadium. He kept his distance for fourteen years. Steinbrenner finally offered an apology and Berra threw out the first pitch in New York's home opener.

"I had to find my way back," Berra said. "I got lost. I've got to get my bearings. It's a lot different. They fixed it up so much."

"I am happy to come in today; I'm glad it's over with. It's good to be back. Everything worked out fine."[37]

It worked out fine after fourteen years, fourteen years in which he was out of contact with the place, the people, and the game he loved. He couldn't bring himself to say "goodbye" to his role with the Yankees. He couldn't imagine his baseball career would ever end. This is in contrast to his oft-quoted philosophy: "It ain't over till it's over," spoken about the game of baseball before the concluding play in the game. Even extra innings do not go on forever.

Most people today know Yogi Berra, not for his baseball career, but for his famous "Yogi-isms," some of which he always contended he never said. He did make this general comment on life: "Ninety percent of it is half mental." What kept him from Yankee Stadium was one-hundred percent mental: his anger, his hurt, his pride. No one suffered more than he did for his refusal to return, in spite of the fact that former teammates attempted to intercede during all those years. Finally, he confessed: "I had to find my way back."

---

37 Quotes from an interview by an Associated Press reporter.

When he did it was the place of a new beginning because he was able to manage a healing ending.

It's Not the Whole Story

Although the book *Never Go Back* is not about loss and grief, there is a line or two that can be applied to endings: "They saw this crisis as one scene in a much longer movie....For successful people, no one event is ever the whole story."[38] At the service for our son, we celebrated the person he was and the many achievements he had made. For his fiftieth birthday celebration, he had assembled a series of large posters picturing his life and work during the half-century. We displayed ten of these for viewing during the visitation at the funeral home. Most people were amazed at his accomplishments and the scope of his talents. He was not defined by his suicide – that was simply a terrible crisis in a much longer story – it was not the whole story.

Yogi Berra let his firing as manager become the entire story of his relationship with the Yankees. He said he got lost. What he lost was the perspective of years of doing what brought joy and meaning to his life. He should have been told by someone: "The one who takes the long view is the one who thrives, no matter what happens along the way."[39] If life is a pilgrimage, there will inevitably be detours and setbacks but they will not be the whole picture of what is happening. I read somewhere of a person being asked their favorite verse of Scripture. The reply was: "It's not just one verse but a recurring phrase throughout the Bible: 'It came to pass....'" The modern version of the phrase is: This, too, will pass."

In the Disney movie *Bambi*, as the fawn and his mother are sheltered in a warm place during a snowstorm, Bambi asks: "Mother, does winter last forever?" We know it doesn't even though in the middle of "the dead of winter" it does feel that way. In the midst of the cold, bitter, painful, and harsh endings in life, we often

---

38 Henry Cloud, *Never Go Back* (New York: Howard Books, 2014), 113, 115.
39 Ibid, 129.

think that things will always be this way. They won't. The promise of Spring is always in the future – even if its arrival is months or, sadly, years away. Nothing lasts forever, which includes the crises.

THERE IS NO SUCH INTERSECTION

One author relates the story of some African pastors who were invited to America for a meeting. They arrive in New York City early and decide to do some sightseeing. When it is time to go to the convention center, they discover they are lost. One of them telephones the center and requests directions for returning. He is instructed to go to the nearest intersection and find the names of the two streets on the signs. His report: "I'm at the corner of 'Walk' and 'Don't Walk.'"[40]

The time between endings and beginnings may lead us to believe we are at such an intersection but that does not name the place where we stand. We need to know how to read the signs and to process where we are and begin to think of how we can get to where we want to go. Being at the corner of "Walk" and "Don't Walk" is to be at a place of paralysis. At a place where we feel there really is nothing we can do. It is the place of hopelessness. The author who gives the above story makes this observation: "It may take this kind of desperate situation for faith to be born in us."[41]

Sometimes the faith required is the confidence that, with God's help, we have done all we can do and it is time to move on. Too many of us are like the auto mechanic in a story someone sent me. Just so you know this is a factual first-person account: it happened at a Chevrolet dealership in Canton, Mississippi. Here is the verbatim account:

> When my husband and I arrived at an automobile dealership to pick up our car, we were told that the keys had been locked in it. We went to the service department and found a mechanic working feverishly to unlock the driver's side door.

---

40 Chuck Queen, *The Good News According to Jesus*, 73.
41 Ibid.

As I watched from the passenger side, I instinctively tried the door handle and discovered that it was unlocked. "Hey," I announced to the technician, "it's open!" His reply, "I know – I already got that side."

The moral is so obvious I hesitate to state it: don't continue to sweat it out after you've done what you ought to do – after you've done all you can do. I often tell congregations that it is possible to move ahead to a new beginning without having every problem fully solved. Wrapping things up is not always neat, tidy, or complete. Complete endings are hardly ever possible. The decision has to be made at some point to close a chapter in order to begin the next one. "Closure" is a term that is sometimes used in the grief process. Better terms suggest being able to reinvest in life and move ahead with lingering pain and questions.

NOT THE END OF EVERYTHING

In the face of the loss of a significant relationship, you may hear the cry, "My life is over." It often feels that way but, finally, if grief is lived with and processed, one realizes that the end of this relationship is not the end of everything. We decide that we can go forward. We decide it is time for a new beginning.

When the children of Israel found themselves exiled in Babylon it must have seemed that everything was over. The Temple had been demolished and the city of Jerusalem was no longer theirs. Psalm 137 is the cry of those who believed everything had ended.

> *By the rivers of Babylon – there we sat down and wept when we remembered Zion. On the willows there we hung up our harps. For there our captors asked us for songs, and our tormentors asked for mirth, saying, "Sing us one of the songs of Zion!" How could we sing the Lord's song in a foreign land?"*
> – Psalm 137: 1-4

The prophet Jeremiah had the unhappy task of convincing the people that this was not the end, that God had a new chapter in mind for his people. The kicker in the promise was that, in the meantime, they were to live out their lives fully in this foreign place. They were to make a total investment in life in Babylon and let God be the author of the new chapter – in his own time. They finally had to get those harps out of the trees and learn to sing the Lord's song where they were.

"In the meantime" is a phrase found often in literature. It generally suggests a great deal that is going on in order to make possible what is to follow. To invest fully in where and how we are is the best way to deal with endings and ensure new beginnings.

And never forget: "Every transition begins with an ending."[42]

AFTERTHOUGHT

The main reason we get trapped in the helplessness state is that we let ourselves become fixed and set into one role, function, work, or relationship and expect that never to become obsolete.[43]

PERSONAL REFLECTIONS

In my eighth decade of life, I'm still working on:

- Knowing when it is time to write "finished" on something that is definitely over.
- Being willing to walk through the grief and pain of the losses that I experience.
- Working very hard at having good endings so that I can have good beginnings.
- Trying to keep in view that endings are but a part of the bigger story of my life.
- Doing the best I can to live in those transition times before a new beginning.

---

42 William Bridges, *Transitions*, 11.
43 Wayne Oates, *The Struggle to be Free* (Philadelphia: Westminster Press, 1983), 127.

QUESTIONS FOR REFLECTION AND DISCUSSION

1. What are the times when it has been most difficult for you to accept that something was truly over?

2. Do you think you give yourself adequate time to mourn the losses you have experienced?

3. Are there any times you have felt yourself at the corner of "Walk" and "Don't Walk?" How did you finally manage to move ahead?

4. Have you ever experienced a time or place when you found it impossible to sing the Lord's song?

5. What do you believe makes it possible to live fully in that barren place between endings and new beginnings?

CHAPTER 5

QUESTIONS ARE MORE IMPORTANT THAN ANSWERS

Then the Lord spoke to Job out of the storm. He said:
Who is this that obscures my plans
with words without knowledge?
Prepare to defend yourself;
I will question you,
and you will answer me. – Job 38:1-3

A CHANGING EMPHASIS

When I began intentional interim ministry, I majored on providing the congregation with answers to most of their questions. The intentional interim involves a self-study divided into five major categories. Over a period of six to seven months, there are many opportunities for my presentations and for small group discussions (eight persons at each table). What I learned through the process of ten years was, not only did I need to help the congregation ask better questions, I also needed to learn how to ask better questions.

Questions have always been a part of our faith-heritage: "Jews pride themselves on being not only the people of the book but the people of the question…"[44] The Bible is full of questions, beginning in Genesis with Cain's "Am I my brother's keeper?" The abundance of questions is quickly discovered as one reads through the Psalms with its writers questioning God's actions, or lack thereof, in their lives. When we get to end of the book of Job, we find the ques-

---

44 Eric Weiner, *Man Seeks God*, 33.

tioning Job confronted by the God who asks questions. Moses not only asks questions, he even questions some of God's announced decisions. Some believe he is the only biblical character who argues with God and wins! (Check this out in Deuteronomy 9:13-19).

Thomas Merton boldly asserts: "In the progress toward religious understanding, one does not go from answer to answer but from question to question."[45] I quickly discovered that the congregations in which it was safe to ask questions were the congregations that reaped the most benefits from the self-study. It also became obvious that disturbing questions resulted in some of the most productive discussions.

WRONG QUESTIONS

Some of you will remember the marketing blunder made by the Coca-Cola company. In the early 1980s, the company was being challenged by the increasing popularity of Pepsi. Pepsi launched a commercial blitz with "the Pepsi Challenge." Coke drinkers were instructed to take a sip from a glass marked Q and one marked M; they were asked which they preferred. The majority chose the M glass – it contained Pepsi. Coca-Cola executives decided that people didn't care for the "bite" of Coke compared with the less harshness of Pepsi. So they decided to launch a lighter and sweeter product; they called it New Coke. This was after conducting countless experiments with a "Coke Challenge." After a sip, most people liked the taste of New Coke better than Pepsi. And away they went.

New Coke was launched and was soon met with an avalanche of protest – even outrage. A few months later, the company came out with Classic Coke, the original formula. New Coke eventually disappeared. How could the marketing experts have made such a miscalculation? Malcolm Gladwell in *Blink* maintains that they asked the wrong question. "Which sip of these soft drinks do you like best?" Gladwell's analysis: "Sometimes a sip tastes good and a

---

45 Tom Stella, *A Faith Worth Believing* (New York: HarperSanFrancisco, 2004), 18.

whole bottle doesn't. That's why home-use tests give you the best information. The user isn't in an artificial setting."[46]

Almost every question has some assumptions in back of it. "A sip will tell us all we need to know" turned out to be a false assumption. Questions do not come from nowhere. Sometimes I ask in a group discussion, "I would be interested in knowing how this has become a question for you. Would you mind telling us its background?" Only then does the group fully understand the question.

RIGHT QUESTIONS

At a Pastors' Conference at Furman University, I heard John Powell give me the right question instead of the wrong one I usually ask myself. In his presentation, he said, "When I got angry in the past, my first question was: 'Why has this person made me so angry? What have I done to deserve such treatment?' Now when anger surfaces I have learned to ask, 'Wonder what is in me that has caused me to respond with such anger to what was said?'"

Dan Bagby in *Seeing Through Our Tears*, provides another wrong/right question:

> "All of us have the power to set limits on God's grace by not allowing it to be active in our lives. The scriptural truth is that we have asked the wrong question. It is not "What can't God forgive?" but "Where have I placed limits on God's grace in my life?"[47]

Both Powell and Bagby provide us with questions that call for reflection and deep soul-searching. These kinds of questions have become far more valuable in my life – if I intend to continue in the conversion process.

Jesus' enemies frequently attempt to trip him up by asking cleverly devised questions. Jesus is asked, "Is it lawful to give trib-

---

46 Malcolm Gladwell, *Blink* (New York: Back Bay Books, 2005), 159.
   Material in the preceding paragraph is also based on Gladwell's book.
47 Daniel G. Bagby, *Seeing Through Our Tears* (Minneapolis: Augsburg, 1999), 38.

ute to Caesar, or not?" Almost every yes or no question is a trap. If Jesus says "Yes," the outrage would have been far greater than the result of issuing New Coke. If he says "No," the Roman authorities will have a solid case against him. Jesus does what he often does in such confrontations: he changes the question. He asks for a coin to be brought and provides a new question: "Whose image is on this coin?" "Caesar's." Jesus' response to his question is: "Give back to Caesar what is Caesar's and to God what is God's." The Gospel accounts of this incident all record that the people who hear *his* answer are amazed. (Mark 12:13-17).

In *Being Mortal*, Atul Gawande provides amazing insight into "Medicine and What Matters in the End" (the subtitle of his book). Much of the book has to do with the manner in which we deal with seniors living in care-facilities. "According to palliative specialists, you don't ask, 'What do you want when you are dying?' You ask, 'If time becomes short, what is most important to you?'" Susan Block, one such specialist, reports that she received a shock when she asked that question. "Well, if I'm able to eat chocolate ice cream and watch football on TV, then I'm willing to stay alive. I'm willing to go through a lot of pain if I have a shot at that."[48]

I am told that the employees of Disney World are taught to respond to the question, "When does the park close?" with "The park stays open until 10:00 p.m." The contrast between the word "close" and "open" does not go unnoticed. A closing-time answer would be stressing the limited amount of time one has left; an "open" perspective focuses on the remaining time to enjoy the park.

ANSWERS TO WHAT QUESTION?

Someone once said, "If you are asking the wrong questions, the answers don't matter."[49] In our culture, we are bombarded with many answers to questions that appear to be crafted for specific

---

48 Atul Gawande, *Being Mortal* (New York: Metropolitan Books, 2014), 182-183.
49 Thomas L. Friedman & Michael Mandelbaum, *That Used to Be Us* (Detroit: Thorndike Press, 2011), 323.

answers. I have always maintained that the one who frames the question has also begun to frame the answer. When an evangelistic effort was launched in America many years ago, its theme was "Jesus Is the Answer." Bumper stickers and billboards were everywhere with this solution to life's problems. One writer maintained: "The message is distinctly unbiblical. The message should be "Jesus is the Assignment."[50] My response to this campaign is the same as David Foster's: "Jesus is just too big for a bumper sticker."[51] Many did scribble on posters that carried the slogan, "What is the question?"

Slogans and catch-phrases are hardly ever sufficient answers to the complex questions that we face. In a *Peanuts* cartoon, Charlie Brown and Pigpen are at the wall having a discussion: Pigpen: "'You never miss the water till the well runs dry.' That's what my grandfather always used to say." Charlie Brown: "He must have been a very wise man." Pigpen: "No, that's all he ever said." This comic strip is really a parable – it calls for a lot of rethinking.

This has often been called "The Information Age." No one has ever referred to it as "The Age of Wisdom." "What I have sensed is an enormous frustration with the unexpected costs of knowing too much, of being inundated with information. We have come to confuse information with understanding."[52]

I agree but would add that a lot of my frustration comes from dealing with people who don't first determine the validity of their sources of information. "Let me tell you what research has proved," does not necessarily guarantee solid information. I need to know what research is being referred to and just how the speaker is interpreting it. Bloggers are ubiquitous and eager to provide "information" on just about everything – and anyone can become a blogger.

If my primary care physician sends me to a heart specialist who suggests surgery, I would not take a poll from the first five persons

---

50 Robin R. Meyers, *Saving Jesus From the Church* (New York: HarperOne, 2009), 120.
51 David Foster, *A Renegade's Guide to God* (New York: Faith Works, 2006), 8.
52 Malcolm Gladwell, *Blink*, 264.

I meet after leaving his office on the advisability of such surgery. If I have doubts, of course, I will consult another heart specialist. The basis on which a person provides information makes all the difference. We need to be able to distinguish between wrong and right questions when we hear them. We need to know the difference between information and propaganda, personal opinion, political rhetoric, or a biased viewpoint. We need to have a large amount of understanding in order to deal with the daily information overload.

AFTERTHOUGHT

Edward de Bono coined the term "lateral thinking." Here is how it might be helpful in our search for better questions (courtesy of Tom Butler-Bowden):

> Lateral thinking is contrasted with "vertical thinking." Our culture in general, but in particular our educational system, emphasizes the use of logic, by which one correct statement proceeds to the next one, and finally to the "right" solution. This type of vertical thinking is good most of the time, but when we have a particularly difficult situation it may not give us the leap forward we need – sometimes we have to "think outside the box." Or as de Bono puts it, "Vertical thinking is used to dig the same hole deeper. Lateral thinking is used to dig a hole in a different place."
>
> To get different results, we need to put information together differently.[53]

PERSONAL REFLECTIONS

In the eighth decade of my life, I'm still working on:

- Seeking fewer answers and asking more questions.
- Trying to discover what assumptions are in back of the questions I'm asked as well as the ones I ask of myself?

---

53 Tom Butler-Bowden, *50 Psychology Classics* (New York: MJF Books, 2007), 39-41.

- Directing more questions to myself and fewer to others as I seek to discover what is going on in a given situation.
- Giving myself the freedom to change a question I feel has already loaded itself with a polarizing answer.
- Reminding myself that the accumulation of knowledge does not necessarily equal the gaining of more wisdom.

QUESTIONS FOR REFLECTION AND DISCUSSION

1. Is there anything about this chapter that makes you uncomfortable? Why do you think this is so?
2. Have you experienced a time when changing the emphasis from answers to questions was more productive? How did this happen?
3. What have been some times when you found it more helpful to change the direction of a question from others to yourself?
4. Have you ever changed a question that you have been asked? What was the result?
5. What do you believe is the difference between information and wisdom?

CHAPTER 6

MYSTERY, PARADOX, AMBIGUITY ARE HERE TO STAY

My God, my God, why have you forsaken me?
Why are you so far from saving me,
so far from the words of my groaning? – Psalm 22:1

DELICIOUS?

Gilda Radner died at age forty-two after a two-and-a-half year battle with ovarian cancer. Shortly before her death, she wrote a book that was published posthumously. Here is her comment on the book:

> I wanted to be able to write on the book jacket: "Her triumph over cancer" or "She wins the cancer war." I wanted a perfect ending, so I sat down to write the book with the ending in place before there was an ending. Now I've learned the hard way, that some poems don't rhyme and some stories don't have a clear beginning, middle and end. Like my life, this book has ambiguity. Like my life, this book is about not knowing, having to change, taking the moment and making the most of it, without knowing what's going to happen next. Delicious ambiguity.[54]

Most of us would have difficulty placing the adjective "delicious" before the word "ambiguity." Dictionary definitions provide other descriptive words: "indefinite," "unclear," "uncertain," "vague." No one wants to think that ambiguous has anything to do with the life of faith. I remember hearing an evangelist loudly

---

54 Patrick Henry, *The Ironic Christian*, 223-224.

proclaim, "I don't have a 'hope-so' faith; I have a 'know-so' faith!" I know the point he was attempting to make but he ought to have added the codicil Paul supplies in 1 Corinthians 13:11: *"Now we see only reflections in a mirror, mere riddles...."* (NJB). The NRSV translation is: *"Now we see in a mirror dimly..."* A footnote on the page tells us: the Greek reads: *in a riddle.*

A NECESSARY TENSION

One of the greatest perils the culture and the churches face today is a growing unwillingness, a fear even, to live within the continuum, in the tension of paradox. We seem to have a compulsion to oversimplify complex problems in order to take action on them....Our inability to discern and tolerate paradox is expressed partly by our growing fear of ideas offered for informed dialogue and debate and the effort to inform ourselves of such dialogue and debate. This tendency is dangerous if only because we can arrive at clear discernment by no other means than dialogue and exchange.[55]

In times of high anxiety people respond too quickly to those who promise to unravel the knots of life's complexities and provide a "know-so" way without any qualifications. In an excellent analysis of Old Testament faith, Rabbi Levi Mejer contends: "Everyone wants security, but nothing can really make us secure, because life itself is a journey into the unknown. Insecurity is at the core of life."[56] The sub-title of his book is: "Using the Stories of the Bible to Improve Our Everyday Lives." Will accepting the truth of the quoted sentence improve our everyday lives? My answer is: absolutely.

---

55 Maggie Ross, *Pillars of Flame* (San Francisco: Harper & Row, 1988), XXXIX, XL.
56 Rabbi Levi Meyer, *Ancient Secrets* (New York: Villard Books, 1996), 22.

It's Biblical

I have a sermon I have preached in several churches (always updated) that I call: "Why Is Life So Unpredictable?" I always provide the printed biblical texts (all NRSV) which we read responsively:

> *Do not boast about tomorrow, for you do not know what a day may bring.*   – Proverbs 27:1

> *Again I saw that under the sun the race is not to the swift, nor the battle to the strong, nor bread to the wise, nor riches to the intelligent, nor favor to the skillful; but time and chance happen to them all.*   – Ecclesiastes 9:11

> *Come now, you who say, "Today or tomorrow we will go to such and such a town and spend a year there, doing business and making money." Yet you do not even know what tomorrow will bring.*   – James 4:13-14a

I begin the sermon with the story of the western horse ranch that has this sign posted as visitors make their way to the corral:

For those who like to ride fast, we have fast horses.
For those who like to ride slow, we have slow horses.
For those who are big, we have big horses.
For those who are little, we have little horses.
For those who have never ridden before, we have horses that have never been ridden.

My comment to the congregation is: We laugh at that and quickly say, "I sure wouldn't take a horse from that last group!" Oh, but you will. And the horse has a name. It is called "tomorrow." And the experience will be unpredictable.

When Steve Friedman asked his father if he had ever been scared serving as a Combat Engineer in the Italian campaign of the Second World War, Sol Friedman said, "I wasn't thinking about the bullet with my name on it. It was the one marked 'To Whom

It May Concern' that worried me."[57] I used that quote in a sermon about the disciples in a boat crossing the lake, Jesus asleep, and the boat being swamped. My comment: Jesus didn't send his disciples into a storm on the Lake of Galilee that had their names on it; what they encountered was a "To Whom It May Concern" storm.

In workshops, I frequently use Ashleigh Brilliant "pot-shots." One of my favorites pictures a man with eyes and mouth wide-open. The caption reads: "Sometimes it seems my whole life is a surprise party."[58] I respond with a comment I once heard: "I resemble that remark!" There have been many surprises in my life of eighty years. Certainly, not all of them unpleasant but all affirming the testimonies of the writers of Proverbs, Ecclesiastes, and James.

William J. O'Malley in *God, the Oldest Question*, in a section titled "Nebulae and Neutrinos, Quasars and Quarks" gives comments I use to end this section:

> The two greatest discoveries of the century – relativity and quantum theory – threw certitude out the cosmic window… Genuine scientists are far more humble than most people naively believe them to be.
>
> Electrons jump orbits without apparent cause…sometimes an electron acts like a pellet but at other times like a wave.
>
> Seekers for God can learn from the practitioners of science, especially in curbing their expectations – and their demands for evidence. Both have to evolve a tolerance for ambiguity, paradox, and polarity – not either/or but both contraries at the same time. Complementarity.[59]

---

57 Tom Brokaw, *The Greatest Generation* (New York: Random House, 1998), 383.

58 Ashleigh Brilliant, *Appreciate Me Now and Avoid the Rush* (Santa Barbara: Woodbridge Press, 1981), 25.

59 William O'Malley, *God, the Oldest Question* (Chicago: Loyola Press, 2000), 51, 56-57.

THEOLOGY IS LIMITED

"Theology is always like having six storm windows to cover eight windows."[60] Alfred Tennyson wrote after his best friend's untimely death:

> Our little systems have their day
> They have their day and cease to be.
> They are but broken lights of Thee
> And Thou, O Lord, art more than they.[61]

Theology as broken lights and a storm window short of adequate coverage are two good metaphors for what those of us with seminary education can bring to our congregations. There are some times when the mysteries, paradoxes, and ambiguities are simply too monstrous for even a meager attempt at clarification.

I will never forget an incident that occurred while I was a pastor in Waynesboro, Virginia. An eighteen-year-old young man (we'll call him Allen, not his real name) who was about to be graduated from high school, bought a new FM stereo radio for his car and drove with a friend to the Blue Ridge Parkway to find out how many stations he could pick up. Night came and they did not return. At three o'clock in the morning the car was found down a mountain side, smashed against a tree. Allen's friend was injured, but survived. Allen was pronounced dead at the scene.

As I sat with the grieving family, the father's cry was, "Why? Why? Why?" The facts were that the curve on the Blue Ridge Parkway where the car went off the road was covered with gravel. The car was probably going too fast for the curve and the tires couldn't maintain traction when they hit the gravel. God didn't send an angel to brush the gravel off the road. The laws of physics were not suspended. Allen's life was snuffed out in an instant. The father kept repeating the phrase, "What a waste!" And he was right. I had no

---

60 William Hamilton, quoted in: Burton Z. Cooper, *Why God* (Louisville: John Knox Press, 1988), 27.
61 Charles E. Poole, *Beyond Broken Lights*, 2.

answer for the question "Why?" I have no answer now. I simply joined with the family as we wept together.

I'm glad no one was there to offer some of the trite theological mantras that one often hears: "We just have to trust that God knows best"; "We finally have to accept that God never makes mistakes"; "God always has a purpose; we just can't see it right now"; "Someday we will understand." I always remember what I once read: "After life falls apart, no amount of explanation can fill the void."

WHERE TO TAKE OUR STAND

I can often imagine Jesus asking me the same question he asked his disciples that day in the boat: "Where is your faith?" (Luke 8:22-25). It has always impressed me that Jesus didn't ask this question while safely standing on the shore; he was in the boat with them. He was in the middle of the storm with them.

These were experienced fishermen. This was not their first storm. They are genuinely alarmed because of its intensity. The account in Luke 8 reads: *"A squall came down on the lake, so that the boat was being swamped, and they were in great danger."* An expanded translation provides a more dramatic picture: *"There came down a whirlwind on the lake, breaking forth out of black thunderclouds in furious gusts, with floods of rain, throwing everything topsy-turvy, and (the boat was) filling with water."*[62] That puts Jesus' question, "Where is your faith?" in proper perspective.

A answer they might have given (probably my answer) is: "To tell you the truth, we didn't expect a storm like this because, after all, you're the one who told us to cross over to the other side of the lake." Many believe that when life is full of trouble and difficulty it is a sure sign they are living outside "the will of God." Here the disciples obey a direct command from their Lord and find themselves in the middle of such a fierce storm that they are in danger of losing their lives. Jesus' question is a call, not for faith that will

62 Kenneth S. Wuest, *The New Testament, An Expanded Translation* (Grand Rapids: William B. Eerdmans Publishing, 1962).

keep life storm-free, but for trust in the middle of whatever life hurls at us. Scott Peck writes: "Faith does not come easily. I still run scared. However, as a result of my minuscule faith I run a little less scared than I used to. Thank God."[63]

Even though most of us probably don't "run scared," too often we live the difficult times with more fear than we would like to confess. It is a continuing struggle: to make peace with the mystery, paradox, and ambiguity that are a part of life; to make peace with the unpredictable that crashes in on us; to make peace with the unexpected that we should expect because it keeps happening.

"Safety and security take back seats to creativity and courage."[64] Or at least they ought to! Trust is very close to courage and demands creativity as we seek ways to move through our present crisis. The faith that sustains us is the trust that the Lord who shepherds us is not only there at the green pastures and still waters but that he is fully present in those valleys that are as dark as death itself. We must truly trust that nothing can ever separate us from his love or his care.

One of the reasons I keep reading Romans Chapter 8 is that it reminds me of some things I need to keep at the center of my faith:

> *The Spirit himself testifies with our spirits that we are God's children. (vs. 16). And we know that in all things God works for the good of those who love him...(vs. 28). If God is for us, who can be against us? (vs. 31). (Nothing) will be able to separate us from the love of God that is in Christ Jesus our Lord. (vs. 39, NIV).*

AFTERTHOUGHT

We are stretched to shift our perspective and our actions from the dualism of either/or to holding the paradox of both/and.[65]

---

63 M. Scott Peck, *Gifts for the Journey* (New York: HarperSanFrancisco, 1995), 68.
64 Judy Cannato, *Radical Amazement*, 139.
65 Angeles Arrien, *The Second Half of Life*, 19.

PERSONAL REFLECTIONS

In the eighth decade of my life, I'm still working on:

- Coming to grips with "not knowing" as normative.
- Including riddles among the many words Paul has given me to describe the life of faith.
- Not ignoring the difficult and perplexing verses of Scripture that challenge a "simple" faith.
- Placing all of my theological knowledge under the category of "broken lights."
- Accepting that many of the things that come my way have "To whom it may concern" written on them.

QUESTIONS FOR REFLECTION AND DISCUSSION

1. Does the material in this chapter make you uncomfortable? Why do you think that is so?
2. Have you experienced any "delicious ambiguity" in your life?
3. Do you feel you have ever ridden a horse named "tomorrow"? What was it like?
4. Do you believe it is contrary to commonly held ideas of faith in God to believe the verses quoted from Proverbs, Ecclesiastes, and James (on page 39)? What is your response to these verses?
5. What would you have said to the father of the young man who died in the automobile accident?

CHAPTER 7

BEING HUMAN IS A BASIC GIVEN

As a father has compassion on his children,
so the Lord has compassion on those who fear him;
for he knows how we are formed,
he remembers that we are dust. – Psalm 103:13-14

THE FIRST WORD

Celebration is the first word that should come to mind when we think about our common humanity. Irenaeus reminds us what should be our first thought when being human is discussed as a liability: "The glory of God is a human being fully alive." At the conclusion of the final "day" of creation, God looked at his entire creation, including human beings, and pronounced *everything* he had made as "very good."

Nowhere in the Bible do we find the Greek idea that our spirits are being held captive in our bodies and the goal is to get rid of the body and achieve perfect spirituality. There is no body/spirit or body/soul division in Scripture. Rather, we are told that when God created human life, he *breathed into his nostrils the breath of life, and the man became a human being* (Genesis 2:7). In the first account of the creation of human life, God says, *"Let us make human beings in our image, in our likeness…".* (Genesis 1:26). Adam does not receive from God anything that Eve does not receive. Both are in the image of God and both have the life breathed into them by the Spirit of God.

Biblically, we do not have a soul, we are a soul. We are not human beings having a spiritual experience, we are spiritual beings having a human experience. We are embodied persons. In Jewish thinking, nothing could be worse than to be a disembodied spirit in Sheol (the abode of the dead). Psalm 30:9-10: *"Therefore my heart is glad and my tongue rejoices; my body also will rest secure, because you will not abandon me to the realm of the dead* (Sheol), *nor will you let your faithful one see decay."* When the Christian Scriptures speak of resurrection it is always of a bodily resurrection. Although Paul won't let people get too specific about exactly what "kind" of a body this is, he continues to maintain: *"There are also heavenly bodies and there are earthly bodies; but the splendor of the heavenly body is one kind, and the splendor of the earthly bodies is another"* (1 Corinthians 15:40).

After the resurrection, Jesus did not appear as a disembodied spirit. Although different in many ways from his earthy body, he asked the disciples to examine the scars left by crucifixion and joined with them in a meal. The witness to the resurrection was: "He is alive! We have seen him!" They were not proclaiming that they simply felt his presence. His presence was once again with them in a bodily form.

Humanity at its Fullest

Some in the early church had difficulty believing that when the Gospel of John states *"The Word became flesh and made his dwelling among us"* (John 1:14), it meant that Jesus became a human being. The New Living Translation provides this translation: *"So the Word became human and lived here on earth among us."* The first heresy the church addressed was the teaching of some that Jesus was not a real human being but only appeared so. The first Christian controversy was not about his divinity, but about his humanity.

Jesus faced a similar controversy in his ministry because he was all too human: *"For John the Baptist came neither eating bread nor drinking wine, and you say, 'He has a demon.' The Son of Man came eating and drinking, and you say, 'Here is a glutton and a drunkard, a friend of tax collectors and sinners.'"* (Luke 7:33-34).

An early Bible study in my first church out of seminary was based on the Gospel of John. In chapter two, Jesus performs his first "sign" by changing water into wine. (The text tells us that Jesus uses the water in six stone jars holding from twenty to thirty gallons. This means that Jesus makes between 150 and 180 gallons of wine - for people who have already done considerable drinking in the days before!) When I finished talking about this incident, a hand began waving near the back of the room and a woman attempted to clarify my teaching: "We all know that was Welchade!" Before I could respond, another woman spoke up: "No! The wedding guests would certainly have known the difference and would not have been surprised that the host had saved the best wine until last. I really believe that Jesus turned water into real wine at that wedding – but it has been an embarrassment to me all my life!"

THE OTHER SIDE OF THE COIN

How many times have we heard (or said), "I'm not perfect; I'm only human." While I trust not excusing unacceptable behavior, it speaks to our limitations, vulnerability, and imperfection. "When you deal with human beings, you have to come to the 'as-is' corner of the universe. (In life's department store) you will find all human beings in the 'slightly irregular' section."[66] That quote comes from the book *Everybody's Normal Till You Get to Know Them*. The title is a play on words and "normal," in the final analysis, means that everyone is fully human. One secret of healthy relationships is relating to all persons "as-is" and accepting that "slightly irregular" is the label on all of us.

The stories that fill the pages of the first book in the Bible are about pretty dysfunctional families. "These are not the Waltons! These people need a therapist!"[67] Abraham attempts to pass Sarah off as his sister, Isaac and Jacob both disrupt their families by making the mistake of choosing a favorite child, Rebecca persuades

---

66 John Ortberg, *Everybody's Normal Till You Get to Know Them* (Grand Rapids: Zondervan, 2003), 13-14.
67 Ibid, 15-16.

Jacob to pass himself off as Esau, Jacob lies to his father and steals the blessing, Joseph's brothers sell him into slavery and lie to their father about Joseph's fate. This is only a sampling of the ways in which these people demonstrate their full humanity. And it is in their full humanity that God leads them and uses them.

Many years ago I purchased a book because of its title: *The Spirituality of Imperfection*. I later attended a Clergy Conference sponsored by a hospital. The topic for the session was *The Spirituality of Imperfection*. The session focused on this factor as a key ingredient in good emotional and physical health and always a needed aspect in ministry. Perfection is not a biblical idea, wholeness is. The call to be "perfect" in Matthew 5:48 is actually the call to be complete as God is complete in his love for all, in making the sun rise on the evil and the good, in sending rain on the righteous and the unrighteous (Matthew 5:45f.) The word *perfect* contains within it the basic themes of wholeness, completeness, maturity, and purpose.

In one of my books, I almost titled a section "Let's Hear It For Imperfection!" but I toned it down to "Imperfection Is Here to Stay." One book written on this subject has this challenge: "This is a book about how imperfect people like you and me can pursue community with other imperfect people....There is no room in Jesus' community for throwing stones. We are all too broken."[68] John Wesley maintained that it is impossible to hold a conversation lasting more than thirty minutes without saying something that shouldn't be said.[69]

Why people outside the church are surprised that people inside the church are human beings is still a mystery to me. No one loses their humanity by walking through the doors of a place of worship. There are many ways this has been stated but none better than what Anne Lamott quotes from a friend who is a recovering alcoholic.

---

68 Ibid, 25, 99.
69 Leonard Sweet, *Out of the Question...Into the Mystery* (Colorado Springs: WaterBrook Press, 2004), 143.

She said that when she'd gotten sober, she saw that even though you get the monkey off your back, the circus never really leaves town.[70]

David Roche uses humor to communicate the same message. I had the privilege of hearing him once in a workshop at Hilton Head. His face is alarmingly disfigured due to a congenital condition. He told the audience that the only difference between us and him is that his imperfection is well exposed on the outside and ours is usually hidden deeply within. He then told us about a church he would like to begin and invited all of us to join. He called it the Church of Eighty Percent Sincerity. He explained: "Eighty percent is about as good as it's going to get....So twenty percent of the time you get to be yourself."[71]

THE BLESSINGS OF AN IMPERFECT LIFE

While perusing the bargain section at a used bookstore (where I always begin), I found a book with the arresting title: *Learning to Fall: The Blessings of an Imperfect Life.* The author, Philip Simmons, was diagnosed with ALS (Lou Gehrig's disease) when he was thirty-five. He describes what living with the disease entails, including "laboring a quarter of an hour to spread cream cheese on a bagel." He writes:

> The challenge is to stand at the sink with your hands in dishwater, fuming over a quarrel with your spouse, children at your back clamoring for attention, the radio blatting the bad news from Bosnia, and say, "God is here, now, in this room, in this dishwater, in this dirty spoon." Don't talk to me about flowers and sunshine and waterfalls: this is the ground, here and now, in all that is ordinary and imperfect, this is the ground in which life sows the seeds of fulfillment. The imperfect is our paradise. Let us pray, then, that we do not shun the struggle. May we attend with mindfulness, generosity, and

---

70 Anne Lamott, *Grace Eventually* (New York: Riverhead Books, 2007), 109.
71 Anne Lamott, *Plan B* (New York: Riverhead Books, 2005), 109.

compassion all that is broken in our lives. May we live each
flawed and too human moment and thereby gain the victory.[72]

Most of us would feel that the word "challenge" is not nearly
strong enough to describe the daily struggles in his life. Most of
us, to a lesser degree, face the same challenge in dealing with our
humanity. It does bring us some comfort to hear about such concepts as "the wounded healer," assuring us that it is especially in our
weaknesses and flaws that we are best able to relate to those in pain.

"I've come to believe that every time I have the compulsion
to put on my Superman outfit and rush to the rescue it's probably
not God talking but my ego."[73] This is from the book *Letters to
New Pastors*. I would add: it doesn't work, either. I have found that
people do not want a super-hero of any kind. They want someone
who can truly empathize; they want someone who can stand with
them on level ground as they deal with life's crises. I truly believe
that it is only in our imperfections, our common bond with all
people, that we are really able to be of any kind of help.

What About the Slips?

"A monk was once asked, 'What do you do there in the monastery?' He replied: 'We fall and get up, fall and get up, fall and get
up again.'"[74] The book cited earlier about a young man with ALS
was titled *Learning to Fall*. It was really about learning to get up.
There are many proverbs about "falling down seven times, getting
up eight." Somewhere I read a statement about the humanity of
saints and that, in spite of all their imperfections, they continued
to "doggedly blunder toward heaven." I have never forgotten that
phrase. When people ask me how I'm doing in my spiritual life,

---

72 Philip Simmons, *Learning to Fall : the Blessings of an Imperfect Life* (New
     York: Bantam Books, 2002), 57.

73 Michael Jinkins, *Letters to New Pastors* (Grand Rapids: William B.
     Eerdmans, 2006), 41.

74 Esther de Wall, *Seeking God* (Collegeville, MN: The Liturgical Press,
     2001), 82.

I reply: "I'm doggedly blundering toward heaven." Which means, every time I fall, I get up.

Planning never to fall, never to fail, never to disappoint ourselves or others, never needing to ask for forgiveness, never having a regret, never letting our imperfections show – is a plan that cannot be carried out. Any attempts result in emotional, psychological, and relational disorders – not to mention the incredible amount of stress that fills our days. Making peace with our own humanity is the first step in accepting others in their humanity.

A Couple of Things to Keep in Mind

Being fully human has been described in many ways and, although no one description captures everything, there are a couple I have found helpful:

> Rumer Godden has written of an Indian proverb or axiom that says that "everyone is a house with four rooms: a physical, a mental, an emotional, and a spiritual." Most of us tend to live in one room most of the time but, unless we go into every room every day, even it only to keep it aired, we are not a complete person.[75]

I interpret this to mean that spirituality involves *all* of life. We do not live in compartments. We are entities without divisions. Our humanity involves everything we are and everything we do.

In her book *The Second Half of Life*, Angeles Arrien gives what she describes as the Four Essential Bones we need:[76]

1. Backbone: the quality of courage, to stand by one's heart or core.
2. Wishbone: the quality of hope, to stay open to dreams, blessings and possibilities.
3. Funny bone: the quality of humor, to foster joy and maintain flexibility.

75 Stephen Bauman, *Simple Truths*, 18.
76 Angeles Arrien, *The Second Half of Life*, 135f.

4. Hollow bone: the quality to trust, to maintain openness, curiosity, and faith.

AFTERTHOUGHT

An indulgence monger, Johann Tetzel (c. 1465-1519) is reported to have said that those who had nothing on their consciences at the time, but had a mind to commit a sin in the near future, could purchase their indulgences in advance.[77]

I can almost hear myself saying, "I'd better take an even dozen."

PERSONAL REFLECTIONS

In the eighth decade of my life, I'm still working on:

- Accepting my being created in the image of God as fully human.
- Knowing that "slightly irregular" is pretty good description of all of us.
- Giving up any idea of having a "perfect day" or a "perfect ministry" or a "perfect anything."
- Realizing that none of us in our local congregations leave our humanity at the door.
- Making the development of my spiritual life totally inclusive of everything that is a part of my life.

QUESTIONS FOR REFLECTION AND DISCUSSION

1. How would you interpret: "The glory of God is a human being fully alive"?
2. Is there anything about the expression of Jesus' full humanity that has ever been an embarrassment to you?
3. How do you see the families in the book of Genesis as "dysfunctional"?

---

77 B. A. Garrish, *The Pilgrim Road* (Louisville: Westminster John Knox Press, 2000), 140.

4.   What do you see as some of the blessings of imperfection?
5.   Are the concepts of four rooms and four essential bones helpful in your thinking about our being human and the development of our spiritual lives?

CHAPTER 8

LISTENING TO MY LIFE IS A DAILY REQUIREMENT

May the words of my mouth and the meditation of my heart
be pleasing in your sight,
Lord, my Rock and my Redeemer. – Psalm 19:14

THE EXAMINED LIFE

I want to think about living and what is important in life, to clarify my thinking – and also my life. Mostly we tend – I do too – to live on automatic pilot, following through the views of ourselves and the aims we acquired early, with only minor adjustments.[78]

This kind of examination is known as reflection. It is, as my dad used to say, a mulling over of things. For me, this is what a great deal of my prayer-life is all about. I begin each day with devotional and biblical reading, ending with Phyllis Tickle's *The Divine Hours: A Manual for Prayer.*[79] This three-volume manual provides scriptures and prayers for three periods of the day and a section to be used before retiring. This saves my prayers from becoming all petition or a litany of woes. The scriptures and prayers I read provide areas for reflection. I always use the morning section and occasionally the others. I have a devotional guide and a Bible

---

78 Robert Nozick, *The Examined Life* (New York: Simon and Schuster, 1989), 11.

79 Phyllis Tickle, *The Divine Hours: A Manual for Prayer* (New York: Doubleday, 2000).

translation new to me (currently an older one by Goodspeed) that I use before retiring.

"The unexamined life is not worth living." Socrates' famous words that come to us from Plato's *Apology* are much easier to recite than to practice. If we are not careful, we allow others to do the examining for us, or, as the beginning quote suggests, follow the views and aims we acquired earlier. You don't have to reach eighty to discover that priorities need constant revision as one moves through the various stages of life. Each period in our lives calls for re-evaluating where we are, what new demands we are called to meet, and what new strategies may be called for.

The Great Themes of Scripture (New Testament) by Richard Rohr is based on talks given as a young priest in 1973. Published in 1988, Rohr confesses in the Forward: "To be honest, I would probably say a lot of things differently now. Then I was young, convicted, surrounded by hope and easy joy."[80]

Rohr wrote the above words only fifteen years after giving the talks. Where we are and how we are brings this kind of confession at many points in our lives. The changing "seasons" of life: infancy, childhood, adolescence, teen years, the education years, the decision years about vocation, young adult, entering the workforce, decisions about marriage and family, adult, the "losing sense of youth" years, middle age, senior years, the time of increasing health challenges, dealing with increasing losses of all kinds, retirement, increasing reflection about time and mortality - all of these seasons call for a new orientation.

In discussing weekly seminars she conducts, Polly Berrien Berends speaks to one of the major goals of reflection: "We tell each other stories, baffling little anecdotes from firsthand experience, and then we look at them in a spiritual light. We try to see what ideas are running our lives."[81] The subtitle of the book is: *Traveling*

---

80 Richard Rohr & Joseph Marton, *The Great Themes of Scripture: New Testament* (Cincinnati: St. Anthony Messenger Press, 1988), vi.

81 Polly Berrien Berends, *Coming to Life* (San Francisco: Harper and Row, 1990), 14.

the Spiritual Path in Everyday Life. Everyday life is where we do our living. Everyday life is where we find our spiritual path. This path is not something reserved for occasions of worship, retreats, or "special times." That is why the examined life – with its everyday happenings – is so important.

WHO'S HOLDING THE CUE CARDS?

The question for this section could just as easily be "Who's in charge of my life?" We not only seek to discover what ideas are running our lives but to whom do we look for spoken or unspoken guidance? Who is holding up the cue cards we are faithfully reading? This is not the question of seeking counsel and advice from persons we trust, it is the question of responding to signals from others about how we should feel, think, or act.

If I am not present as the watcher of my mind, my thoughts, my emotions, and my reactions, I can get in a whole lot of trouble.

> Two men are out driving and run into each other. The first climbs out of the wreckage of his car and helps the second man, who is badly shaken, to the side of the road. "You had a nasty shock," he says, and offers a hip flask to the other man, who takes a long, grateful gulp. "Go on, have another." "But what about you?" asks the second man. "Don't you drink?" "No," replies the owner of the hip flask. "Not until after the police arrive."[82]

When I used this story in another book I wrote this comment: "I don't want to believe that all the people who try to push our buttons are as deceptive as the man in this story but they are usually not focused on our well-being. They are more concerned about themselves than they are with us".[83]

Whether it is waving cue cards or attempting to manipulate our response, it all amounts to being "other-directed" instead of

82 Jimmy Carr and Lucy Greeves, *Only Joking* (New York: Gothan Books, 2006), 197.

83 Ronald Higdon, *But If Not*, 211.

"inner directed." This is the simple way to describe the difference between assuming responsibility for our own lives and permitting others to be in the driver's seat. I first found the phrase "watcher of your mind" in this short paragraph:

> Be present as the watcher of your mind – of your thoughts and emotions as well as your reactions in various situations. Be at least as interested in your reactions as in the situation of person that cause you to react.[84]

Unfortunately, I recall many times when I focused almost completely on the situation or the person who was "causing" my problem. I often jokingly say, "One of the great secrets of life is knowing who to blame." Biblically, this philosophy goes all the way back to the Garden of Eden: Adam blamed Eve and Eve blamed the serpent. Listening to my own life and discovering what is in me that is causing me to react in a given manner is an on-going challenge because: "Self-knowledge is never procured cheaply."[85]

The toughest thing I do in any situation is to accept that I am responsible for how I respond. Listening to my life during times of crises and conflicts is especially instructive. Once I stop pointing the finger at others and look inward, I have at least taken the first step to being able to choose my own response.

What Will the Neighbors Think?

My mother would on occasion ask this question when our behavior as children had not been quite what she wanted for our reputation in the neighborhood. We do care what other people think. Growing up, it is especially our peer group that we usually seek most to please because we want to "fit-in." The problem with "What will the neighbors think?" as a life motto is that it leaves much of our criteria for living in the hands of others.

---

84 Eckhart Tolle, *The Power of Now* (Novato, CA: New World Library, 2004), 55.

85 Michael Casey, *Toward God* (Liguori, MO: Liguori/Triumph, 1996), 5.

There is another aspect to this approach captured in the phrase "If you live for applause, you'll die by applause."[86] It hit me especially hard because it comes from a book titled *Letters to New Pastors*; I think we never outgrow the need to heed that warning. Those of us in the helping professions, and especially ministers, have the desire to be people pleasers. We want to be loved and accepted. We want people to like us. In order to be a pastor it is necessary to build good relationships with the members of your congregation – but not at the price of your integrity. Not at the price of opting for approval over authenticity. Plus, I think Alan Alda's father was right in the advice he gave him: "I learned from my father that if you're just looking to take bows, you'll always be disappointed because the applause is never loud enough."[87]

"Jesus never worshiped at the altar of human approval. But we sure do."[88] I would like to believe that I never worshiped at this altar, but I have. And it has always gotten me into trouble. If human approval guides your life you will have to be careful never to rock the boat, never to say things that are too challenging, never wander off into the shocking requirements of the gospel, never wander into the deep water of prophetic truth (that must *always* speak that truth in love). In reality, the attempt at conflict avoidance in the church usually results in more conflict. Conflict, of course, is inevitable in the life of any relationship.

Side-bar: Being an intentional interim minister calls for helping people deal openly and redemptively with the conflicts that are preventing their congregation from moving forward. I always devote one full session of our study to the subject of conflict. The specifics of that would require another book but I attempt to lay the groundwork for discussions in many other sessions on how we can keep conflict at the level of "a problem to solve" and not allow

---

86 Michael Jinkins, *Letters to Young Pastors*, 107.
87 Alan Alda, *Things I Overheard While Talking to Myself* (New York: Random House Trade Paperbacks, 2008), 83.
88 Paul Couglin, *No More Christian Nice Guy* (Minneapolis: Bethany House, 2005), 83.

it to escalate into destructive character assignation and arriving at intractable positions.

When Is Enough Enough?

Listening to our lives is almost impossible unless we find ways to turn down the volume of everyday living. I confess up front, that I do enjoy turning up the volume on my sound system when I am watching an action movie (another confession to being a movie buff – from whence has come many sermon illustrations!). This does not mean that I want *all* of life to be digital seven-channel sound with a built-in woofer. That does seem to be the case, particularly in college sports. In attending a local college football game, I took note that the one repeated sign held up by the cheerleaders and flashed across large screens was "Get Louder!" How one can get louder for almost three successive hours is beyond me, although every effort is usually made to do so. I recently saw an ad for a concert series that was titled "Louder Than Life." I can only imagine, with throbbing eardrums, the level of the music at that event.

What I am about to say must not be taken as the words of a luddite. I am the blessed beneficiary of many technical marvels. What I do protest is the belief that with our new and ubiquitous means of communication we are required to stay connected 24/7. Seeing families at a restaurant eating dinner, with the younger members talking on cell phones, texting (even another person at the table!) or perusing the Internet is disturbing. Sometimes the entire family is involved. For all healthy relationships there must be times of face-to-face, fully focused, conversation. There are times when we have to disconnect in order to really connect.

You can't really listen to your own life or to the lives of others without turning down the volume – without frequently hitting the off button. Staying connected takes a heavy toll both in automobile crashes and the crumbling of relationships with those who matter most to us. I often ask, "How much louder can things get?" It's already loud enough to drown out conversation in restaurants, time for quiet and reflective moments in physician's offices, and leisurely shopping free from mind-jangling accompaniment. (Does sound almost like a luddite, doesn't it?!)

PUTTING DOWN AN ANCHOR

Creating periods of relative silence is not an option if I intend to provide the setting in which it is possible to do some inner-listening. It is necessary for another reason: "Putting down an anchor or two amid the swells of each day is essential if we are to avoid bobbing on its surface or being washed away by its demands."[89] The quiet time that begins my day makes all the difference in the way I am able to deal with what follows. When I get too busy to take an adequate amount of time in the morning for stillness and reflection, I can tell the difference in my day. It should be instructive to all of us that the Gospels record Jesus withdrawing many times from the crowd and even spending all night in prayer. Much of that prayer time I believe was in reflection, meditation, and listening.

An incident reported by a father illustrates what we are after:

> My nine-year-old son, Jackson is a mystic in the making. We were walking a path along the River Thames as it leaves Oxford, England. After a half hour of quiet, he turned to me and said that taking a long walk into the woods is "like opening the envelope of your soul – an envelope that is usually sealed up tight." To further explain he said, "It gives you a chance to concentrate...." And then he stopped and said, "No, that's not quite right. In fact, it's exactly the opposite. When you're out here, you're really not concentrating even though your mind is working It's like you are aware of important things without even happening to try. Your envelope is opening."[90]

I read somewhere of South American tribe that regularly scheduled times of rest in any journey so that their souls could catch

---

89 Dorothy Bass, *Receiving the Day* (San Francisco: Jossey-Bass Publishers, 2000), 37.
90 Robert B. Kurschwitz, ed., *Attentive Patience* (Waco: Baylor University, 2016), 28.

up with them. Britain's Royal Navy has a practice known as the "all-still." When there is any kind of serious problem, the captain announces an all-still and for three minutes no one is allowed to move or speak. The writer who is my source for this information, then comments: "Three minutes of silence and stillness can have exponential effect in the middle of a turbulent situation."[91]

Let's go from three minutes to three days. I attended a Mercer University Preaching Conference in 2009 where Kyle Matthews told about a friend of his who went on a three day silent retreat at the Abbey of Gethsemani in Kentucky where Thomas Merton lived and is buried. His friend is a sound engineer. When he returned and Kyle asked him how it was he said, "Dude, after two days of total silence, you start to hear things!"

In the front lobby of the guest house of the Abbey of Gethsemani there is a register that has a column for "Observations." Under the heading are the most eloquent arguments for the benediction of silence:

> A return to the deep well of peace.
> I came to talk, discuss and argue. I learned to listen.
> For once I let God do all the talking.
> A welcome comma in my life.
> Beyond words.
> A point of stillness in the search for the stillpoint.
> Ahhhh![92]

Instead of an "amen," I close this chapter with one of my favorite movie quotes: "So let it be written! So let it be done!"

Afterthought

When life throws us a curveball, our instinct is to react by picking up the phone and calling five of our friends to vent. We almost invariably regret this as the dust settles. Our first response

91 Matthew Kelly, *The Rhythm of Life* (New York: Fireside, 2004), 203.
92 Greg Levoy, *Callings* (New York: Three Rivers Press, 1997), 30.

should be to take the situation and our feelings about the situation to the classroom of silence.[93]

PERSONAL OBSERVATIONS

In my eighth decade of life, I'm still working on:

- Making a regular time each day for meditation and reflection.
- Taking time periodically to attempt to discover what stories are running my life.
- Recognizing when I am being other-directed rather than inner-directed.
- Keeping "people pleasing" from preventing my being authentic.
- Taking times in the midst of a demanding schedule to stop and let my soul catch up with my body.

QUESTIONS FOR REFLECTION AND DISCUSSION

1. Is there anything in this chapter that was a wake-up call in your life? What do you plan to do about it?
2. Name those who in the past have held the cue cards for you. Why do you think you allowed them to do so?
3. Have you had Alan Alda's experience of overhearing things while talking to yourself? What kind of discoveries did you make?
4. Do you find the volume of life turned up too loud? How do you cope with the noise pollution?
5. Do you have regular times of putting down anchors "amid the swells of each day"? What do you do? How do you do it?

---

93 Matthew Kelly, *The Rhythm of Life*, 73.

CHAPTER 9

TRUTH IS A JOURNEY OF DISCOVERY

Show me your ways, Lord,
teach me your paths.
Guide me in your truth and teach me.... – Psalm 25:4-5

WHAT IS TRUTH?

Pilate is not the only one to ask, "What is truth?" (John 18:38). Those who believe they can answer his question are ubiquitous. The most outrageous example from one of these "answers" comes from a person in an educational institution who was asked how he would dialogue with those who held different opinions on certain subjects. His reply was: "Dialogue? If you have the truth, what is there to dialogue about?"

The implications of that response hardly require any unpacking on my part. The relationships that have been broken, the bridges that have been burned, the isolation and polarization that have been created, the general overall destruction that has resulted, and the blood that has been spilled all too frequently come from those believe they are in possession of the truth. There is still considerable debate about whether truth is something one can "possess." Although I probably will be hinting at what I believe about this issue, I leave the philosophy majors to deal with that one in all its complexity.

> When we claim to have arrived at the Truth, capital T,
> we cheat ourselves. Finality of understanding, closure of inter-
> pretation, shuts one off from further insights, illuminations,

inspirations, etc. When it comes to Truth with a capital T, we spend our lives in waiting rooms on our knees. There are no "immaculate perceptions." We all walk in the dark.[94]

There is no more glaring example of an "immaculate perception" than the refusal of other scientists and philosophers to look through Galileo's telescope in order to see the "proof" of his assertions. Professor Guilo Libri, a philosopher, was one of those who refused to look. When asked why, he replied that there was no need to do so because he had the truth already.[95] The Pope was furious when Galileo published his book *Dialogue Concerning the Two Chief World Systems.* Thirty-two years earlier, "Giordano Bruno had been burned at the stake for merely suggesting that the Universe might be infinite, in opposition to contemporary interpretation of Holy Writ."[96]

A Discovery or a Journey?

There is not enough space in this brief chapter to list all of those who maintain that truth is a journey of discovery. Here are two:

> If God were to hold out enclosed in His right hand all Truth, and in His left hand just the active search for Truth, though with the condition that I should ever err therein, and should say to me: "Choose!" I should humbly take His left hand and say: "Father! Give me this one; absolute Truth belongs to Thee alone."[97]

From some source which I have lost, comes a phrase I frequently use in workshops: "I have a point of view; you have a point of view; only God has view." Absolute truth belongs to the only

---

94 *Homiletics*, April-June 1995, p. 10.

95 Len Fisher, *Weighing the Soul* (London: Weidenfield & Nicholson, 2004), 32.

96 Ibid, 33.

97 G. E. Lessing, *The Oxford Dictionary of Quotations*, Third Edition (Oxford: Oxford University Press, 1979), 314.

One able to see it. All the rest of us see in a mirror dimly (1 Corinthians 13:12). This does not mean that we live without any truth or that we have failed to grasp some essential truths. From the same chapter in his letter to the congregation in Corinth, Paul says, For we KNOW in part (emphasis mine). There are some things we do know. We simply do not believe we have discovered the whole truth; we know, but we know in part.

"Any one truth is not the whole truth; if we are in danger of being submerged in partial truth, the remedy is to cling to its opposite."[98] I don't go quite that far but in workshop discussions. I do often ask the question: "That is true but what else is also true?" Our acknowledgment and acceptance of the partiality and incompleteness of our grasp of the truth is a prerequisite for entering into any kind of dialogue.

Sir Isaac Newton:

> I do not know what I may appear to the world; but to myself I seem to have been only like a boy playing on the seashore, and diverting myself in now and then finding a smoother pebble, or a prettier shell than ordinary, whilst the great ocean of truth lay all undiscovered before me.[99]

A minister of another generation, Ralph Sockman, gives the concept an added dimension: "The larger the knowledge, the longer the shoreline of wonder."[100] And most are familiar with Thomas Edison's observation: "We don't begin to know one percent about ninety-nine percent of anything."[101]

How Much Truth?

If Jack Nicholson's famous response from the witness stand, "You can't handle the truth!" means you can't handle all the truth, it

---

98 Michael Casey, *Toward God*, 109.

99 John Bartlett, *Familiar Quotations*, 14th Edition (Boston: Little, Brown, and Company, 1968), 137.

100 John Ed Mathison, *Treasures of the Transformed Life*, 137.

101 M. Scott Peck with Marilyn Von Waldner, *Gifts for the Journey*, 41.

has a biblical basis. Jesus informed his disciples, *"I have much more to say to you, more than you can now bear. But when he, the Spirit of truth, comes, he will guide you into all truth"* (John 16:12-13). My free translation: "There's a lot more that you don't know but there's no way I'm going to dump the whole load on you – you would be crushed. Later, when the Spirit comes, he will assist you in your journey into truth."

In the sixteenth century, George Herbert gave a warning that I wish many of today's pontificators could hear: "Be calm in arguing; for fierceness makes error a fault and truth discourtesy."[102] The political campaigns we have endured for the past year have been overflowing with discourtesy. I hardly ever hear in the media anyone *speaking the truth in love* (Ephesians 4:15). Aristotle gave the most famous receipt for honesty with style: "The right truth… To the right person…At the right time…In the right way…For the right reason."[103] "Well, it's the truth!" is no reason that it must be spoken. People who pride themselves on constantly dishing out the truth (as they see it), speaking their minds on all occasions, always leave behind a trail of wounded and hurting survivors, victims of their artillery of truth.

A part of courteous truth involves not making it a frontal assault. Emily Dickinson put it this way:

Tell all the Truth but tell it slant…
Too bright for our infirm Delight
The Truth's superb surprise!
The Truth must dazzle gradually
Or every man be blind.

---

102 G. E. Lessing, *The Oxford Dictionary of Quotations*, 247.
103 Lewis Smedes, *A Pretty Good Person* (New York: Harper and Row, 1990), 79-80.

Perhaps it can best be summed up in Christopher Morley's analogy: "Truth is not a diet, but a condiment."[104]

JUST BELIEF?

"I have no greater joy than to hear that my children are walking in the truth" (3 John 4). I have always felt that "believers" is too small a word to describe those of us in the Christian faith. I get a few raised eyebrows when I say, "If what you believe doesn't make any difference in the way you live, then it doesn't matter what you believe." There is certainly content to our faith but that content must find a way to begin to shape our everyday lives. *Walking in the truth* implies that it is a part of our pilgrimage. Truth is not just a discovery, it is a journey of discovery that is not confined to pleasant and familiar roads. Neither is it confined to places where I am convinced I will find truth. Truth often comes from unexpected places and people. Nathanael's question, *"Can anything good come out of Nazareth?"* (John 1:46), is one that continues to be asked. "How could this place, this person, have anything of value to offer me?" The answer Philip gave to Nathanael is the one he gives to all of us, *"Come and see."*

While working in one of his fields, an old Kentucky farmer, was called to by a young man standing on the side of the road. It turned out the young man was spending his summer selling books. He had one he was certain the farmer could use: *New and Better Ways of Farming*. He was not deterred when the farmer shook his head and said, "Not interested." "Aren't you interested in being a better farmer?" The response that silenced him: "Son, I'm not farming now as well as I know how."

There is much truth we know that we are not able, by either ability or choice, to put into practice. "The trouble with the truth is that, once we see it and know it, it might demand more of us than we can comfortably give."[105] I believe that is especially true for bib-

---

104 Gorton Carruth and Eugene Ehrlich, *American Quotations* (New York: Wing Books, 1988), 567.
105 Charles E. Poole, *Beyond the Broken Lights*, 5.

lical truths like those found in the Sermon on the Mount (Matthew
5 – 7). It certainly demands more than most of us can comfortably
give. My question: Is truth supposed to make us comfortable and
feel at ease? Are not the truths that challenge and disturb us the very
truths we need in order to bring about necessary changes in our
lives? *Walking in the truth* will certainly take me into some pretty
rough terrain and up some very steep inclines.

I close this chapter with an anonymous prayer from an ancient
scholar:

From the cowardice that shrinks from new truth,
From the laziness that is content with half-truths,
From the arrogance that thinks it knows all truth,
Oh God of Truth, deliver me.[106]

Afterthought

In the movie *International Hotel*, W. C. Fields lands his plane
on the roof of a hotel somewhere in China. He asks where he is
and is told, "Wu Hu." "I'm looking for Kansas City," he announces.
"You are lost, sir!" someone shouts. "Whereupon, with something
of arrogance and conceit, he raises his head, throws out his chest,
and says, 'Kansas City is lost; I am here!'"[107]

Personal Reflections

In my eighth decade of life, I'm still working on:

- Recognizing that each day is another day for my truth journey.
- Reminding myself that, although I do have a point of view,
  only God has view.

---

106 Angeles Arrien, *The Second Half of Life*, 128.
107 Gordon B. Hinckley, *Standing for Something* (New York: Three Rivers
    Press, 2000), 41.

- The timing of speaking the truth: the right truth, to the right person, at the right time, in the right way.
- Attempting to walk in the truth of which I am already aware in order that I may be open at some point to new truth.
- Making the prayer from an ancient scholar with which this chapter closes, one of my daily prayers.

QUESTIONS FOR REFLECTIONS AND DISCUSSION

1. Which of the concepts in this chapter have you found the most difficult to deal with? Why?
2. Have you ever refused to look through a telescope for fear of what it might do to your beliefs?
3. Have you ever been the victim of discourteous truth? How did you handle it?
4. What do you think it means to tell truth at a slant? How have you heard it done?
5. Why do you think truth is so often simply taken to mean what one believes? Why do you think there is not more emphasis on the biblical admonition to walk in the truth that one professes?

Chapter 10

Perseverance May Be the Most Important Ingredient in Life

*Hope in the Lord
and keep his way.* – Psalm 37:34a

One Day At a Time

During an especially stressful time in my ministry, my wife found a small ceramic magnet that she placed on the front of our refrigerator. It read: "I'm going to quit. But not today." I naturally read this several times each day and it spoke to me on a couple of levels. First, it was the reminder that I had the option of stepping out of my situation. I never felt trapped but realized if things got so bad that I felt it was over, I could announce, "I'm out of here." Ironically, that is one of the things that kept me from quitting.

Second, I was also reminded of how important it is to live in day-tight compartments. I knew I could not endure the stress of my situation if I tried to absorb it a month at a time. I did feel I could make it through another day. This is not unlike the philosophy AA provides: The goal of an alcoholic is to live this day sober. I took as my mantra the Vacation Bible School motto I had used many years earlier: *"This is the day the Lord has made; let us rejoice and be glad in it"* (Psalm 118:24; NRSV).

Fortunately, during all this time I never stopped seeking out pieces of humor to lighten the load. My weekly browsing in the bargain section of Half Price Books placed in my eager hands *Unwritten Laws* by Hugh Rawson. The subtitle is: *The Unofficial Rules of Life as Handed Down by Murphy and other Sages.*[108] Almost everyone is familiar with Murphy's Law: "If anything can go wrong, it will." Some of the other "laws" simply provided a reason to smile: Ade's Law: "Anybody can win, unless there happens to be a second entry." Cayo's Law: "The only things that start on time are those that you're late for." McGregor's Revised Maxim : "The shortest distance between two points is under construction."

AN UNFORESEEN BLESSING

Some of the unwritten laws from this book gave me much more than a smile. For example, Laingren's Law: "Human beings are like tea bags. You don't know your own strength until you get into hot water." A major blessing during this time was the generous gift of one of the members of my congregation for sessions with a pastoral counselor. During these sessions, I was able to discover many things about myself that would have probably continued to remain buried had not the current situation called for their unearthing.

Perseverance has always been a little easier for me when I have been able to keep believing that in my wilderness experience I might be able to hear things that the times of "success" had drowned out. "Is there anything I can learn from this experience?" is always the question to ask in almost all of our conflicts, but especially in times of major crises. It seems only then that we are able to be open to things that challenge our usual attitudes, philosophies, and approaches.

I can testify that "Change occurs at the edge of complexity."[109] Smooth, rather uncomplicated times, allow for smoother sailing. There is no need to risk being prophetic or suggesting radical challenges to others or ourselves. But when things get thick with complexity, the situation changes because we are called to change. And like the frog in the rut story mentioned earlier, we change be-

---

108 Hugh Rawson, *Unwritten Laws* (New York: Castle Books, 1997).
109 Bob Sitz, *Not Trying Too Hard* (Washington: Alban Institute, 2001), 237.

cause we have to. My confession is that, as I look back on my life, I have made significant changes only because I had to.

PATIENCE?

A most unfortunate (and incorrect) translation has given many people a mistaken picture of Job. James 5:11 in the King James translation reads: *"You have heard of the patience of Job."* Whenever I read that, I always wanted to shout, "No I haven't! On every page of his story, Job is pitching a fit. He is complaining about the injustice of what has befallen him and can't understand why his friends keep maintaining his guilt when he knows he is innocent of any wrongdoing that deserves such calamities. He can hardly wait to get his chance to ask God some questions!" Every translation since then renders the verse: "You have heard of the perseverance of Job." When reading that, I can say, "Yes, I have heard of that." Job's wife wants him to curse God and die. That he won't do. He insists on preserving and he does.

In describing the fruits of the Spirit in Galatians 5:22, the Greek word Paul uses for *patience* "is most properly translated as 'a conquering endurance.'"[110] This is also the best description of perseverance I have ever read. *Endurance* in the Bible can almost always be translated as *perseverance*. To endure is not simply to roll over and be the victim of whatever life is dishing out. As in Job's case, there is always some element of protest, some element of challenge, some element of determination not to roll over and play dead, some element of determination to get through what is happening, some element of clinging to the possibility of wringing victory out of seeming defeat.

Henri Nouwen: "The word 'patience' means the willingness to stay where we are and live the situation out to the full in the belief that something hidden there will manifest itself to us."[111] It is noteworthy that this quote comes from a book titled *Attentive Patience.*

---

110 Daniel G. Bagby, *Seeing Through Our Tears*, 138.
111 Robert B. Kurschwitz, ed., *Attentive Patience*, 79.

DETERMINATION

"Sir Winston Churchill…delivered his former high school's shortest commencement speech when he stood up, stared intensely into the student's faces and shouted: 'Never-never-never-never-never give up!'"[112] When one gives up, it is the announcement that all is over, things are finished, you intend to make no more effort in the struggle. Rare, I trust, are those occasions when this is necessary.

"Rev. Hal Noash, a pastor of a church where I interned in Dallas, once said, 'The greatest ability you can have today is stickability.'"[113] This gives perseverance an everyday tag that almost everyone understands. My dad always instructed, "Stick to your task until it is completed." Having stickability ensures that we are bringing to life the ability to see things through to a conclusion.

Much is accomplished also in us when we have this quality. James 1:4: *"Let perseverance finish its work so that you may be mature and complete, not lacking anything."* The lessons and disciplines that assist us to maturity and completeness don't come without a great deal of stickability and conquering endurance. It also calls for what one writer describes as *"spiritual isometrics."*

> I encourage what I call *spiritual isometrics*. Isometrics is a way of exercising by pitting one muscle against another, like putting a clenched fist in the palm of the other hand and pushing and resisting with full strength. Spiritual isometrics is the practice of pitting our prayerful thoughts against the circumstances of the day.[114]

In no sense do I ever suggest that perseverance is simply a matter of waiting things out. None of life, I have found, calls for a passive stance. Even a decision not to take any action at the present time, comes from remaining engaged.

---

112 Daniel G. Bagby, *Seeing Through Our Tears*, 139.
113 Doug Herman, *What Good is God?* (Grand Rapids: Baker Books, 2000), 57.
114 J. Ellsworth Kalas, *The Pleasure of God* (Louisville: Westminster John Knox, 2016), 28.

Another aspect of perseverance that I find especially enlightening, comes in the form of a question: "Do you have the patience to wait till your mud settles and the water is clear? Can you remain unmoving till the right action arises by itself? Tao Te Ching."[115] This is another reason for taking time for reflection. The slogan I have seen, "Don't just do something. Stand there!", doesn't always sit well with an action-oriented culture. "There's always something we can do," is a consistent plea. However, we all know that the right action at the right time often comes with clarity that is not immediately ours. As with so many things in life, timing can be everything.

THE SOLUTION

I have never had more response to a story than the one I am about to relate. Shortly after I used it in a Sunday morning sermon, an attorney who was a member of our church, informed me that he used it in a court case.

The story is told of a golf course in India. Apparently, once the English had colonized the country and established their businesses, they yearned for recreation and decided to build a golf course in Calcutta. Golf in Calcutta presented a unique obstacle. Monkeys would drop out of the trees, scurry across the course and seize the golf balls. The monkeys would play with the balls, tossing them here and there.

At first, the golfers tried to control the monkeys. Their first strategy was to build high fences around the fairways, and the greens. This approach, which seemed initially to hold much promise, was abandoned when the golfers discovered that a fence is no challenge to an ambitious monkey. Next, the golfers tried luring the monkeys away from the course. But the monkeys found nothing as amusing as watching humans go wild whenever the little white balls were disturbed. In desperation, the British began trapping the monkeys. But for every monkey they carted off, another would

---

115 Wayne Muller, *Sabbath*, 169.

appear. Finally, the golfers gave in to reality and developed a rather novel ground rule: Play the ball where the monkey drops it.[116]

This calls to mind what I recently read in *Being Mortal*: "We were up against the unfixable. But we were desperate enough to believe that we weren't up against the unmanageable."[117] Working within the "givens" of any situation is always the way out of the frustration of attempting to control or change what is beyond our power. After I used the golf story, many times I heard people say, "Well, you'll just have to play the ball where the monkey drops it." I knew what they meant.

AFTERTHOUGHT

When tough times arrive, they usually overstay their welcome, so be patient.[118]

PERSONAL REFLECTIONS

In my eighth decade of life, I'm still working on:

- Trying my best to live in day-tight compartments that enable me to achieve something just for today.
- Attempting to learn what difficult and stressful times can teach me.
- Making certain my endurance is not passive but one that keeps me fully engaged.
- Having patience to wait until some clearance comes as to what action I ought to take.
- Believing that although things are not "fixable," they are always to some degree "manageable."

---

116 Gregory Knox Jones, *Play the Ball Where the Monkey Drops It* (New York: HarperSanFrancisco, 2001), 3.

117 Atul Gawande, *Being Mortal*, 223.

118 Chriswell Freeman, *When Life Throws You a Curveball, Hit It* (Nashville: Walnut Grove Press, 1994), 13.

QUESTIONS FOR REFLECTION AND DISCUSSION

1. Has there been a time when you wanted to quit and didn't? What was the result?

2. What unforeseen blessings have you found in some of your darkest times?

3. How do you see the quality of "stickability" in your life? In what ways has it paid dividends?

4. How would you respond to Churchill's commencement speech?

5. What are some of the ways in which you have been able to manage things that were not fixable?

Chapter 11

I am Called to be the Best Version of Myself

Create in me a pure heart, O God,
and renew a steadfast spirit within me. – Psalm 51:10

I Gotta Be Me

Recently, I have read several books emphasizing God's call to each of us to become the best versions of ourselves. This has little to do with the philosophy of the popular Frank Sinatra song, "I Did It My Way." That may or may not be the best version of who we are. It sounds far too "selfie" to be a very healthy approach to personal development.

"Why do so many of us think that being one's self almost never implies being one's best self? Why is it that when we let it all hang out we are often rude, insensitive, noncommunicative, unkind, uncaring?"[119] In this case, "letting it all hang out," amounts to opening the Pandora's box of a totally undisciplined life. I do believe God's calling is for me to be the self that most reflects what it means to have been created in the image of God.

A Better Motto

One writer tells of a youth camp that had this posted motto: "My own self, at my very best, all the time."[120] While not in any

---

119 Joseph L. Roberts, Jr., *Sideswiped by Eternity*, 64.
120 David Gregory, *How's Your Faith?* (New York: Simon & Schuster, 2015), 182.

way an achievable goal, it remains worthy of being a daily pursuit. The author who cites this motto, earlier makes a confession: "Anger has always been my adversary, crouching just outside the door. We cannot make our adversaries disappear. All we can do is to refuse to let them in."[121] My problem is I always seem to leave that door open – just a crack!

Being the best version of ourselves requires continuing discipline and course correction. It does not mean overcoming of humanity but embracing a humanity that is fully alive in the best sense of that word. My wife has told me that she has selected her epitaph and that she is serious about it. Here it is: "All things considered, she did pretty well." Perhaps that ought to be the addendum for being the best version of ourselves: being the best version of ourselves - all things considered. This has nothing to do with making excuses or taking the easy way out (my wife has done neither) but admitting that many factors make it impossible to be all that we really feel we should be and are trying to be.

This emphasis on who we are as persons seems crucial to me in the light of eternity.

> At the end of his last official speech as director of the USIA (United States Information Agency), defending the principle of truth-telling even when discussing our worst flaws, he reminded his listeners that appearances finally don't count for much. "At the end of the day," he said, "it's what we *are* that matters."[122]

Whenever anyone quotes the play and movie title of some years ago, *You Can't Take It With You*, as a reminder of all we leave behind, I always have a rejoinder: "But you can! You take *everything* with you! You take yourself. You take all that you are. You take everything that you have become." The irony is that we spend entirely too much time on the things we are going to leave behind and too little on the one thing we *can't* leave behind: ourselves. The

---

121 Ibid, 134.
122 Geoffrey C. Ward, *American Originals*, 152.

most important thing when I get ready to leave this world is the person I have become.

AN INDIVIDUAL UNIQUENESS

I remember hearing John Powell at a Pastor's Conference at Furman University ask a question I have never forgotten: "If I'm not going to be myself, who am I going to be?" Then he talked about the various pressures that others brought to his life about things he ought to do, changes he ought to make, ways in which he ought to be different that in no way reflected who he was. He was not suggesting that he paid no attention to how others saw him, but that, first of all, he was called to maintain his integrity – his uniqueness.

I have repeatedly said that whenever we choose approval over authenticity we are in trouble. We are not being true to ourselves, to our best selves. In every congregation I have served there were always people who wished I were more like another pastor they had had. One couple where I was pastor had moved from Texas and never forgave me for not being a whiz-bang like their Texas minister. And I'm here to tell you he was one whiz-bang! I knew him and found him to be a little "too much" for me. This no way implies that he was not authentic or that he was not a great pastor to many people (his churches had been much larger than mine – remember, this was Texas). It was almost as though this couple was asking me to make a complete personality change – to become somebody I wasn't.

I almost titled a section in this chapter "Unrealistic Expectations Are Unrealistic." One of the final things in each interim self-study is a "Pastoral Expectations Survey." From a list of about forty-five qualities, each person is asked to select twelve they would most like the new pastor to major on at the beginning of ministry with their congregation. They are asked not to rank the twelve. Almost everyone agrees that no pastor could possibly meet all forty-five expectations. We discuss how expectations change over time and need periodic discussion and re-evaluation.

The problem is that too many expectations are not openly acknowledged or shared with a pastor. "I thought every pastor would know that," speaks to an unvoiced expectation. I always told a congregation new to me that, in packing for my move to this pastorate, I had accidentally broken my crystal ball so I would have to depend on them to give me any information they felt I should have. This didn't solve all problems but I did use it as a reminder when anyone said to me, "Oh, I'm sorry, I thought you knew that."

There is also the problem of expectations I simply cannot fulfill because they do not represent gifts I possess or I do not feel are a part of my calling. And if you want to discover the true meaning of exhaustion, just attempt to meet everyone's expectations. This will keep you so thin and so scattered that you will find it difficult to give very much time to those things you feel are your definite calling.

COMPARISONS

I remember reading of one person's nightmare. He was standing in line where credentials for heaven were being checked and he found himself behind Mother Teresa. He clearly heard the Lord say to her, "You really could have done a little more." If that became my reality, I would simply step out of line. In no way could I ever stand the test if I were compared to Mother Teresa. The big question is: am I called to be a Mother Teresa? Am I called to the same kind of ministry that was hers? If I am going to be compared to the great saints it might be better just to quit now.

Although the Bible does teach about a day of accountability (commonly known as Judgment Day), nowhere is there the suggestion that evaluation forms are going to be passed out and the Lord will use them for the basis of his evaluation. Romans 14:12 tells us: *"So then, we will give an account of ourselves to God."* I am not going to be asked to give my opinion on the life of anyone other than myself. I am not going to be judged in comparison with anyone else. The parable of the "talents" (Matthew 25:14-30), which is really about the investment of money, clearly teaches that we will be called to account for our faithfulness in what has been entrusted to us, the gifts we possess, the particular calling that belongs to us. Luke 12:48 is the none-too-gentle reminder: *"From everyone who has been given much, much will be demanded...."*

In his *Confessions,* Andrew Greeley, a Catholic priest and author, writes:

> Fortunately for me, my parents' emphasis on effort rather than outcome – and powerful praise for effort – dispensed me permanently from the obligation to be perfect. So I was freed by my parents, to a considerable extent anyway, of the need of perfectionism and of envious resentment of those who were better than I was – wonderful blessings because they have made it easy to distinguish between myself and my work.
>
> I am not James Joyce (or) Agatha Christie....In fact, one could fill the pages of a book with a list of authors and artists that I am not. But so what? Why need I be any of those people? And more to the point, why should my work be evaluated against theirs? I write the kind of stories that I like to write, stories which I design to be comedies of grace.... Why is it necessary to be Graham Greene or James Joyce? Why isn't it enough to be me?[123]

THE BEST VERSION OF MYSELF WHEREVER

"I remember a struggling college fraternity brother saying before Christmas break he was going to Colorado to find himself. When he got back in January, we asked him how his trip to find himself went. He said, 'I went to Colorado to find myself, but I wasn't there.'"[124] The all too obvious response to this is: we only find ourselves where we are because that is where we are. In my

---

123 Andrew Greeley, *Confessions of a Parish Priest* (New York: Simon and Schuster, 1986), 46-47.
124 Henry Cloud, *Never Go Back*, 190.

present context, among my current relationships, in the midst of all my limiting circumstances – here is where I am called upon to be the best version of myself. Nothing is possible in Colorado that is not possible right here and now.

In a comment alluding to the 1924 Olympics and Eric Liddell's classic comment in *Chariots of Fire*: "God made me for China but he also made me fast…and when I run *I feel his pleasure*," this observation: "As to say, 'God made me thus, and when I so live, I feel his pleasure.' It follows that anything which cannot be lived with such holy gladness should not be a part of one's life."[125] It should be noted that the subtitle of the book from which this is taken is: *Finding Grace in the Ordinary*. The author does not cite the 1924 Olympics in his reference but attempts to make an application to everything that makes up the ordinary experiences of our daily lives.

Being the best versions of ourselves will hardly ever be very spectacular or on a very large stage. (The dangers inherent in both of these can only be imagined.) The call is to be our best wherever we are. Huston Smith met this challenge in a most unlikely place. On May 31, 2009, he turned ninety and soon found himself in an assisted-living facility. In his book *Tales of Wonder* he confesses that: "The first night after the move was a dark night of the soul. Religion relies on that successful plot device, the happy ending. I still believed in one, but…I thought the happy ending will now have to wait until I am dead. And then after three days…it became acceptable, perfectly fine."[126] I have no doubt it would take me much longer than three days to get over this kind of a dark night of the soul. But, then Smith tells us how he was able to do just that.

> People go to nursing homes, I've heard it said, to die. I came to this assisted-living residence, it seems, to cheer people up. I still begin each day with exercise for the body, reading religious classics for my mind, and prayer for the spirit.…I have added a fourth practice. Mentally I take a census of the

125 J. Ellsworth Kalas, *The Pleasure of God*, 5.
126 Huston Smith, *Tales of Wonder* (New York: HarperOne, 2009), 177.

other residents here, and as each appears in my imagination, I ask how I might improve his or her day.[127]

Believing we have a calling to live out the will and purpose of God wherever we are is one of the secrets of being able to fully invest in life – of being able to commit ourselves to being the best version of ourselves. Years ago, I remember reading about a woman who found herself in the hospital for what promised to be a rather lengthy stay. She reports asking herself, "I wonder what God has for me to do here?" She believed there was always something to be done even in a hospital setting. So do I.

AFTERTHOUGHT

I have found these "Never-Go-Back-Awakenings" particularly helpful as I continue to pursue becoming the best version of myself.[128]

1. Never again…return to what hasn't worked.
2. Never again…do anything that requires you to be someone you're not.
3. Never again…try to change another person.
4. Never again…believe that you can please everyone.
5. Never again…choose short-term comfort over long-term benefit.
6. Never again…trust someone or something flawless.
7. Never again…take your eyes off the big picture.
8. Never again…neglect to do due diligence.
9. Never again…fail to ask why you are where you are.
10. Never again…forget that your inner life determines your outer success.

PERSONAL REFLECTIONS

In the eighth decade of my life, I'm still working on:

---

127 Ibid, 179.
128 Henry Cloud, *Never Go Back*, 13.

- Carefully evaluating whether, in trying to be myself, I am truly working on being my best self.
- Placing the major emphasis on what I am becoming as a result of my philosophy and behavior.
- Not regretting that I do not have the gifts of a whiz-bang minister.
- Attempting to use to the best of my ability the gifts God has given me.
- Making every effort to find and do God's will for me in every time at every place.

QUESTIONS FOR REFLECTION AND DISCUSSION

1. Have you ever been to "Colorado" to try to find yourself? What did you discover?
2. How do you conceive of "accountability" day?
3. How has it felt when someone has compared you with another who has far greater gifts?
4. How have you responded to the unrealistic expectations that have been placed on you?
5. Where have you found it the most difficult to believe that God still had something for you to do?

CHAPTER 12

CONVERSATION/DIALOGUE IS ESSENTIAL IN ALL OF LIFE

How good and pleasant it is
when God's people live together in unity! – Psalm 133:1

THE CURRENT SITUATION

> Our communication model is broken. In this consumer culture we've been trained to accept ad slogans, labels, sound bites, and bumper-sticker slogans as adequate. These micro-blips of information reduce the complexity of an issue, strip essential meaning from it and ultimately snuff out conversation.[129]

In this election year (2016), my only response to this paragraph is "Amen!" If you are reading this, it means I survived what many are considering the worst example of political "discourse" in our nation's history. The question "How much worse can it get?" is usually answered nightly on the national news with clips of outrageous rhetoric unlike anything we have ever heard. It certainly looks as though conversation has been snuffed out.

This is the most obvious illustration of something that I believe has taken place in too many of our relationships – some would go far as to use the adjective "all." How much genuine conversation have you experienced in your family, in your work place, in your

---

129 Dan Merchant, *Lord, Save Us From Your Followers* (Nashville: Thomas Nelson, 2008), 121.

place of worship, in your community, or in the political structures of your local and state governments? Case closed.

Is This What We Really Need?

Our local newspaper has a regular section underneath "Letters to the Editor" titled "Rants and Raves." Even though this is frequently what is done in the letters, this space is especially caustic. There is also a website "justrage.com" that permits you to have a scream or two to reach those beyond your local hearers. It is described as the "internet anger sponge" but (I just checked it out) it reads more like the venom scatter gun. I didn't read very far until I had enough rage residue to require a mental clean-up!

The real problem with "Rants and Raves" and "justrage.com" is that they are not intended for dialogue. The ranter, raver, and rager appear to have no desire for any kind of healing conversation for their emotional tirade. The value seems to be all in the process of venting their side of the argument which is the only side. At times, it goes beyond being right and wrong; it becomes a battle between good and evil. It is the "we take no prisoners" approach. I cannot find anything helpful or redemptive in any of these approaches.

In every intentional interim where I have served, the first order of business is to turn down the heat. I need to create a better atmosphere in which to be able to talk about the issues that have become so inflammatory that discussion has become practically impossible. This is one of the reasons an intentional interim minister is called first to be "a non-anxious presence." It is the first step in helping to cool things off. I'd like to see a section in the newspaper devoted to "Calmer Expressions of Positions" and a website called "justlisten.com."

It seems an almost impossible task, but my purpose in congregations has been the same as this author's goal for his book: "My goal in this book is to drain some of the heat, anger, and divisiveness out of these topics and replace them with awe, wonder, and curiosity."[130] I was immediately drawn to the book because of its subtitle: *Why Good People Are Divided by Politics and Religion.* In my work, I find that good, sincere people become mired in destructive conflict they had no intention of creating. They are just not able to understand why others cannot see they are right! (The title of the cited book at the beginning of this paragraph is: *The Righteous Mind*).

THE PLACE TO BEGIN

"To live without listening is not to live at all; it is simply to drift in my own backwater."[131] Joan Chittister (one of my favorite speakers and authors) has some insightful things so say about listening. Chapter Two in her book, *Wisdom Distilled from the Daily: Living the Rule of St. Benedict Today,* is titled: "Listening: the Key to Spiritual Growth." From that chapter:

> The spiritual life is achieved only by listening to all of life and learning to respond to each of its dimensions wholly and with integrity....It is one thing to try to hear what is in front of us. It is another to willingly expose our ideas to the critical voice of a wiser heart...We must all learn to listen to the truths of those around us.[132]

What I learned in the process of my work as a church consultant is that my first responsibility is to listen to the congregation. That is never easy because it is so obvious they need to hear so many things from me! After all, think of the training and experience that have brought me to them! When you begin speaking before listening you have ensured that your words will fall on deaf ears – not because they do not want to listen but because they are not able to hear you. All conversation begins with listening.

---

130 Jonathan Haidt, *The Righteous Mind* (New York: Pantheon Books, 2012), xii.
131 Joan Chittister, *Wisdom Distilled from the Daily*, 21.
132 Ibid, 16, 19.

"Listening itself communicates the value of the other person and (their) thoughts, so the act of listening is an act of love... Related to listening is something that a mentor of mine described as 'giving space' to people."[133] Listening is the necessary beginning of conversation. It says, "You are a person worth hearing and your thoughts are important to me." "What do you know?" is the message a person gets (whether spoken or not) when we refuse to listen. Respect for the other, regardless of how we feel about the position they have taken, is always the first step in attempting to begin healthy dialogue.

I would like to post this Native North American proverb in a prominent position on the wall in the room where I am conducting a workshop: "Listen, or your tongue will keep you deaf."[134] (I only use illustrative quotes that do not require explanation!) Henry Ford gave listening a practical twist: "If there is any secret of success it lies in the ability to get the other person's point of view and see things from their angle as well as your own...And if you do truly see it the other person's way – deeply and intuitively – you might even find your own mind opening in response."[135]

Here is a helpful suggestion for better listening: "A good question to ask those who have a different point of view: 'Help me understand what you mean by it.'"[136] The author of this suggestion then comments:

> Jesus had no problem, apparently, with a dialogue across quite varied traditions: the good Samaritan, the Samaritan woman at the well, the Syro-Phoenician woman, centurions, Nicodemus. The only ones he couldn't crack were the single-minded exclusivist temple elders. ("Our view is the truth; thus yours must be false. Heresy and error have no rights.")[137]

---

133 Adam S. McHugh, *Introverts in the Church* (Downers Grove, IL: IVP Books, 2009), 98.
134 Marcus Braybrooke, *Life Lines*, 105.
135 Jonathan Haidt, *The Righteous Mind*, 49.
136 William J. O'Malley, God: *The Oldest Question*, 81.
137 Ibid.

The All Too Obvious

Nothing takes the place of face-to-face conversation. The secret of successful workshops I soon discovered was to seat the group at tables of eight and provide plenty of time for this kind of small group face-to-face discussion. Through the years many people told me, "We've never done anything like this in our church before! We've usually had 'town forums.'" In one church, I had to spend a considerable amount of time helping the congregation recover from a recent town forum. It was basically a "forum" dominated by the strongest personalities and voices with the tone of "Now hear this!" People were exhausted when the ninety-minute session was over. And the divisions were even more pronounced.

I don't believe it is possible to have a conversation in a room with seventy-five to one hundred people. First, they are usually seated in rows. Even though the speaker may move to the front, people are not close enough to catch many of the unspoken aspects of communication; they are also unable to observe the facial and bodily responses of the other listeners. We all acknowledge that words are not the only part of communication. Robert Bolton: "The common estimate given in research papers is that 85 percent of our communication is non-verbal. Therefore attending skills, which are about the extent to which we are "there" for someone when they are speaking, are vital to good communication."[138]

My primary responsibility is creating a safe place for the honest exchange of ideas. "In a good focus group, participants are made to feel comfortable talking about what they truly think and feel."[139] "Honesty and empathy are the cornerstones of connection: honesty about what is going on in ourselves and empathy for others."[140] It usually takes several months before people begin to feel safe enough to "open up." To do so, they have to know they will not be ignored, ridiculed, rejected, demeaned, isolated, or demonized for

---

138 Tom Butler-Bowden, *50 Psychology Classics*, 34.
139 Frank Luntz, *Words That Work* (New York: Hyperion, 2007), 77.
140 Deborah van Duesen Hunsinger, *Bearing the Unbearable* (Grand Rapids: William B. Eerdman's, 2015), 109.

what they think or believe. They have to know they will be taken seriously. They have to know they are seated at a table of "empathetic listening."

My first rule of thumb in personal relationships is: "Say how you feel and ask for what you want." This "works" because it is free from any attack on the other person, it sends only "I" messages, it begins not with "facts" but how we feel about what has gone on, and it makes a request which opens to the door for discussion and (hopefully) compromise. (You may not always get what you want but it puts something specific on the table.) Whenever I suggest this, the complaint often comes that it is too simplistic. When I ask how often the questioner has used this approach, I get only a head-shaking. I stress this is the place to *begin* because it does not put the other person on the defensive.

In small group discussions this approach can be of great value in helping people understand each other. Following a workshop session, I often hear: "I never knew he/she felt that way." This is all a part of listening to one another's stories. If I don't know something about your story, I cannot begin to understand why you believe some of the things you do. With increased understanding comes increased acceptance. Every safe place for conversation is characterized by openness and acceptance.

THE TYRANNY OF E-MAIL

This is the title of a book by John Freeman that provides "The Four-Thousand-Year Journey to Your Inbox." In another chapter "Life on the E-mail Treadmill" he writes:

> The truth is that text rarely, if ever, can equal the richness of a face-to-face conversation. It's static, disembodied. It does not convey hand gestures, verbal tone, inflection, or facial expressions, things we are taught from birth to encode and decode.[141]

---

141 John Freeman, *The Tyranny of E-Mail* (New York: Scribner, 2009), 106.

This is not to mention texting, Facebook, Twitter, blogging, and other ways of connecting without really connecting at all. These provide words without context, words in isolation from the necessary ingredients for conversation, and words that often lead to further isolation. My plea is not for the abandonment of these tools but for the placing of them on the back burner when one wants to truly communicate. It is a plea to disconnect in order to connect. Statistics reveal: "The tone of e-mails is misunderstood more than half of the time, compared to just a quarter of the time over the phone and even less often face-to-face."[142]

Among the ten recommendations Freeman offers are these:

- Don't check it first thing in the morning or late at night.
- Check it twice daily.
- Read the entire incoming e-mail before replying.
- Do not debate complex or sensitive matters by e-mail.
- If you have to work as a group by e-mail, meet your correspondents face-to-face.
- Schedule media-free time every day.[143]

AFTERTHOUGHT

Helpful suggestions almost always must be concrete. Frank Lutz in *Words That Work* gives ten rules of effective language. Here is a summary:

- Simplicity. Use small words.
- Brevity: Use short sentences.
- Credibility is as important as philosophy.
- Consistency matters.
- Novelty: offer something new.
- Sound and texture matter.
- Speak aspirationally. Warren Beatty: "People will forget what you say but they will never forget how you made them feel."

142 Ibid, 107.
143 Ibid, 206f.

- Visualize. Paint a word picture.
- Ask a question.
- Provide context and explain relevance.[144]

(Read his excellent book for a full discussion of each.)

PERSONAL REFLECTIONS

In my eighth decade of life, I'm still working on:

- Turning down the heat, anger, and divisiveness to whatever extent I can in whatever situation I find myself. (And encouraging awe, wonder, and curiosity).
- Trying not to join the rant and rave mob – even though I have to do it on occasion – in private!
- Majoring on listening before I do any speaking. This is especially difficult for us "talkers."
- Requiring face to face conversation before I discuss any important or sensitive issue.
- Not checking my e-mails more often than three or four times a day. (I haven't yet reached Freeman's suggestion of only twice a day).

QUESTIONS FOR REFLECTION AND DISCUSSION

1. How much genuine conversation do you hear on a daily basis? Where does it occur most offer and why?
2. What was your reaction when you viewed the "justrage.com" website?
3. Which of the suggestions for listening do you find the most difficult to put into practice? Why do you think this is so?
4. What is your response to the "Say how you feel and ask for what you want" suggestion?
5. Which of the ten rules for effective language speak loudly to you?

---

144 Frank Lutz, *Words That Work*, 4f.

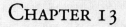

CHAPTER 13

THE FIRST WORD IS GRACE;
THE LAST WORD IS GRACE

Give thanks to the Lord, for he is good.
His love endures forever. – Psalm 136

(The phrase, *his love endures forever,* is repeated twenty-six times in this psalm.)

IN ALL AREAS

I still have a copy of the series of lectures John Powell gave many years ago at a Furman University Pastors' School - its title: "Grace as a Life-Style." Powell applied grace to every area of our lives with biblical and life illustrations that I have never forgotten. For him, grace permeates all of life and gives the courage to face whatever comes our way. It is telling that at the conclusion of this series he delivered to about five-hundred pastors, he received a standing ovation. We all needed that blessing of grace.

Grace has traditionally been defined as "unmerited favor" but it is much larger than this. Biblically, grace is something that cannot be earned; it is God's gift to us. Grace means unconditional love. Grace means total acceptance just as we are. Grace comes without qualification, judgment, or limitation.

In sermons on the subject, I have often used two phrases: the first is, "We need to get off God's payroll and into his blessing plan." If you are on God's payroll (of course, this is not really possible), God is limited as to what he can give you. You get exactly what you have earned. Some of Jesus' most outspoken opponents believed they were on God's payroll and that they were among his best paid workers – because they deserved it. The book of Job is written in protest to the philosophy of Deuteronomy: if you are good you will be protected and blessed – if you do wrong you will be punished. Job's three friends are not the only ones to believe this is the way the world works, that it is the only thing that makes sense. The truth is, in the light of reality, it doesn't make any sense at all.

The second phrase I use is: "Nothing good I do causes God to love me more; nothing bad I do causes God to love me less." To illustrate the absurdity of the opposite of this position, I ask, "What would be your reaction if I told you that, because I had been especially good for several weeks, I decided it was time to pray for something really big?" After all, I was simply going to cash in on the merit account I had built up. Deuteronomy 10:17 warns us: *"For the Lord your God is God of gods and Lord of lords, the great God, mighty and awesome, who shows no partiality and accepts no bribes."*

As a recovering alcoholic, one young man told me this "second phrase" (in the above paragraph) helped to change his life. The concept needs much unpacking but Psalm 136 is only one of the many places where God's grace, mercy, and love for us are proclaimed as consistent throughout our lives, period. This is not meant to suggest that there are no consequences for irresponsible, selfish, and destructive behavior. This is not meant to suggest that this is a license to live anyway one chooses. (Paul deals with this in his letters in no uncertain terms.) But it does mean that God's faithfulness can be counted on no matter what. That assurance is needed especially when we know we have missed the mark and fallen far short of the glory God intends for our lives.

A Universal Need

Ernest Hemingway wrote a story about a Spanish father who decided to reconcile with his son who had run away to Madrid. Now remorseful, the father took out an ad in *El Liberal* newspaper: "Paco, meet me at the Hotel Montana noon

Tuesday. All is forgiven. Papa." Paco is a common name in Spain, and when that dad went to the square he found eight hundred young men named Paco waiting and hoping for their fathers.[145]

I can only imagine how many are dying to hear the words "all is forgiven" in order to restore some broken relationship. Often, the only solution to hurt, misunderstanding, and alienation is forgiveness. This is the solution found in the story of Joseph and his brothers. Nothing else can make things right in the sense of bringing about reconciliation. There is no way to "fix" the injustices of Joseph's behavior as the favored son or the wicked deeds of his brothers. There is enough blame to go around for everybody (which is usually the case). The only answer to all the wrongs is forgiveness.

"The greatest benefit of forgiveness: for both persons, forgiveness means the freedom to be at peace inside their own skins and to be glad in each other's presence."[146] I will add another: forgiveness creates a new future. It provides the freedom to go ahead. It removes the roadblocks and the fills in the potholes. It means that tomorrow really is another day. Jesus had much to say about forgiveness, much that seems impossible. This includes the number of times we are to forgive (seventy times seven) and the illustrations in his own ministry of the persons to whom he offered immediate and absolute forgiveness – even when there is no record of some even asking for it! The greatest gift of grace is its accompanying forgiveness. Forgiveness is the lifeblood of all relationships.

In commenting on the first part of Romans 8:1, *"There is therefore now no condemnation...,"* one writer says, "These are truly the most beautiful words ever spoken or written, either in the Bible or in any other literature."[147] In the margin of the book I wrote "Yes!" There is not a one of us who doesn't long to hear the words

---

145 Michael E. Brown, *Bottom Line Beliefs* (Macon: Smyth & Helwys, 2009), 56.
146 Joseph L. Roberts, Jr., *Sideswiped by Eternity*, 150.
147 Lance Webb, *Conquering the Seven Deadly Sins* (New York: Abingdon Press, 1995), 124.

Jesus spoke in John 8:11: *"Neither do I condemn you."* Even though this incident is not in the earliest manuscripts, it certainly seems illustrative of all that is recorded about Jesus' ministry. He lived out the Gospel writer's contention that God did not send his Son into the world to condemn the world... (John 3:17). Grace may bring us to confrontation with many of the things we need to face in our lives but it never leaves us with condemnation.

For most of us, the greatest difficulty in the gospel of grace is the acceptance of the fact that we are accepted. Many of us spend a great deal of time attempting to earn acceptance. It is difficult to receive, what for me, is this greatest gift of grace: I accept that I am accepted. I accept myself. Self-acceptance continues to be a struggle for most of us because we know ourselves too well. But God's grace has nothing to do with accepting us in spite of what and how we are but in the fullness of who we are right now. You don't have to clean up your act for God's grace, forgiveness, and acceptance to be yours. It takes me an entire sermon to unwrap this concept: forgiveness *precedes* repentance. We repent *because* we are forgiven and accepted; we do not repent in order to *be* forgiven and accepted.

However...

There is one phrase that provides the great "however" in any discussion about grace:

> First of all, if human freedom is genuine and God really did give us genuine autonomy when God called us into being, and if love is noncoercive, how can you unequivocally assert that everybody is going to do a certain thing? Grace isn't a bulldozer that finally makes people do something, whether they're willing or not.[148]

---

148 John Claypool, *Stories Jesus Still Tells: The Parables* (New York: McCracken Press, 1993), 61.

If grace were a bulldozer, it wouldn't be grace. It is always an offer. It is always an invitation. It is always a gift that is waiting to be received. It is always ours for the taking. But God is not going to kick down the front door and come charging into our lives. I don't have to earn grace but neither will it be forced on me.

William Archibald Spooner (1844-1930) is the patron saint of all of us who remember embarrassing tongue-tangled pulpit moments. Spooner frequently reversed the initial letters or syllables of two or more words in his Anglican sermons. "A crushing blow" became "a blushing crow" and "I have a half-formed wish in my mind" became "I have a half-warmed fish in my mind." These slips of the tongue came to be known as "spoonerisms." In a sermon emphasizing how "the Lord is a loving shepherd," the congregation was informed that "the Lord is a shoving leopard."[149]

My comment on that is always: "If Satan prowls about like a roaring lion (I Peter 5:8), then perhaps God might be more effective as a shoving leopard." But it would *not* be effective for what God seeks to accomplish in our lives and in his world. I fear that too many of our attempts to share our faith have taken the shoving-leopard approach. If we feel we must make an offer people cannot afford to refuse, we have adopted the god-father approach. The darkest part of Christian history illustrates the destructive power of this philosophy and of its on-going consequences.

Grace Meets Us Where We Are

The Gospels provide the best illustration of this truth. Another illustration comes from a book you may have trouble finding. I found it in a place I will not mention because when I recommended it to another minister and he went to find it in a similar store in his city, he was asked, "Why in the world would any minister want to read that book?" It was no longer available in that location. I told him I would secure a copy from my store, but when I went to get

---

149 Ronald Higdon, *From Fear to Faith*, 122.

another one, I was informed it had been pulled from the shelves. I now find myself in possession of a banned book which is too much for many to take. So, if you feel you must skip over this next brief section, that's okay.

The book to which I am referring is Dan Merchant's *Lord, Save Us From Your Followers*. It is not for the faint of heart or for those who don't want to learn what many outside the church think of us. Many parts of it are pretty far out but, as such, provide much food for thought. The jacket reads: "Bumper Sticker Man, Dan Merchant, armed with a microphone and a film crew, becomes a battlefield correspondent in the culture war. His mission? Find out why the gospel of God's love is dividing America."

Dan put on his bumper-sticker suit (the stickers run the gamut) and went to Times Square in New York City to strike up conversations with strangers by asking them five questions: (1) How do you think the universe began? (2) Where do you think you'll go when you die? (3) Name something Jesus Christ is known for. (4) Name something the Christian people are known for. (5) Do you know what the phrase "culture wars" means?[150] Consistently, in response to question three, people named positive things about Jesus and, in response to question four, only negative things about his followers (selective hatred and intolerance are two examples). He talked to people very few Christians would ever approach and he did so in the form of questions in order to discover where and how they were. He went places and talked to people many would label "outrageous." Jesus' opponents appear to have offered similar ongoing criticism of his ministry. He was in the wrong places with the wrong people. For many, Dan Merchant and his book are just too much.

CAN GRACE GO TOO FAR?

There are two major illustrations in scripture of when people believe grace has gotten out of line. The first comes from Jonah

---

150 Dan Merchant, *Lord, Save Us From Your Followers*, 2-3.

when he is outraged that God has forgiven the Ninevites and decided not to bring judgment on them. "The amazing grace of God was a little too amazing to suit Jonah."[151] The second illustration comes from Jesus' parable of the vineyard owner who pays the same wage to everyone who works for him, regardless of the number of hours. When those who have worked all day complain that they did not receive any more than those who worked only one hour, the owner of the vineyard has a question for them: *"Are you envious because I am so generous?"* (Matthew 20:15).

The parable in Matthew 20 is not about labor relations, it is a parable about the Kingdom of God (the Kingdom of heaven) or, better, the reign of God. It is about God's generosity and his refusal to measure out or limit his grace. We have a tough time with grace that is without boundaries. We may not deserve grace but surely there are some who deserve it a whole lot less! We feel like the elder brother of the prodigal: how could his father throw a party for his worthless brother who did nothing but squander his inheritance in wild living while he faithfully, and dutifully, worked like a slave? It just isn't fair.

"We can't bundle grace. Grace is too big. But say we were granted superabundant arms and could. The needle on the scale would fly off the top and ricochet into the universe."[152] There's nothing very amazing about most people's concept of grace – the good people get it and the really bad people don't. And we've been checking the list; we know who's been naughty and who's been nice. The author who gives the quote that begins this paragraph, says in a sermon: "My central message today – the good news that I bring – is that we live in the power of superabundant grace."[153]

If it were not superabundant, if it were not too big to bundle, if it were not too much for any scale to measure – it wouldn't be the kind of grace any of us need. It wouldn't be the kind of grace

---

151 Charles E. Poole, *The Flute Beneath the Gold* (Macon: Smyth & Helwys, 2002), 66.
152 Mary Carthlegehayes, *Grace* (New York: Crown Publishers, 2003), 113.
153 Ibid, 114.

that goes too far – which is where the prodigal son found himself living (in the far country) and where most of us find ourselves at one time or another. The grace that goes too far is the only kind of grace that reaches far enough for all of us.

THE GREATEST BENEFIT OF GRACE

Perhaps the greatest benefit of grace is that it enables us to live with gratitude. Most who write books on "successful" aging, list one of the major requirements as gratitude. G. K. Chesterton gives this advice for living a life of gratitude:

> You say grace before meals. All right. But I say grace before the play and the opera. And grace before I open a book. And grace before sketching, painting, swimming, fencing, boxing, walking, playing, dancing. And grace before I dip the pen in ink.[154]

Life is a gift. Everything in it is a gift. Chesterton simply acknowledges all these gifts by not simply confining his "saying of grace" to mealtimes. From a lost source, I have the story of one little girl at Thanksgiving time who was asked to tell what she was most grateful for. She thought long and hard. Then she said, "I am thankful that I am thankful." Since some have labeled our culture "the culture of complaint," when one is thankful, this is indeed something for which to be thankful.

Meister Eckhart, the Christian mystic, asserted that if the only prayer we ever prayed our whole life was "Thank You," that would be enough.[155]

AFTERTHOUGHT

Being grateful implies a perspective that is continually on the lookout for blessings and is not focused on the life's negatives. I often term this "the attitude of gratitude." In a workshop, I heard

---

154 J. Ellsworth Kalas, *The Pleasure of God*, 5.
155 Wayne Muller, *Sabbath*, 128.

a new twist on the old saying, "As you ramble through life, dear friend, whatever be your goal, keep your eye upon the donut, and not upon the hole." The speaker told about a minister who used that phrase in a workshop. He was elaborating on what this means, when an angry woman yelled out in frustration, "You should see the size of the problem I have to deal with." The minister's response: "In such a case, the answer can only be: the bigger the hole, the bigger the donut."

Personal Reflections

In the eighth decade of my life, I'm still working on:

- Trying to develop grace as a life-style.
- Daily confessing my need for forgiveness.
- Investing in the future by working on forgiveness of others.
- Seeking to avoid at all costs using the bulldozer approach.
- Refusing to ever bundle or limit grace even for the most "undeserving."

Questions for Reflection and Discussion

1. Was there anything in this chapter that presented a real challenge?
2. What do you think of the idea: "Nothing good I ever do causes God to love me more; nothing bad I do ever causes God to love me less"?
3. How easy has it been for you to accept that you are accepted?
4. Have you ever felt genuine sympathy for the elder brother of the prodigal and for those who labored in the vineyard for twelve hours and received no more that those who had worked a single hour? Why do you think this is so?
5. Is the concept that forgiveness precedes repentance new to you? What do you understand this to mean?

Chapter 14

There's Got To Be More

But God will redeem me from the realm of the dead;
he will surely take me to himself. – Psalm 49:15

"Let's Wrap It Up"

That phrase is used when the time has come to pull things together and write finished on a project. Hopefully, it signals that everything necessary has been done and there are no loose ends. The wrap-up is announced because there is a sense of completion. It brings the same satisfaction a writer has when "The End" can finally be written.

Were it only so with life! I don't believe one ever reaches the point of no loose ends or ever achieves the feeling of completion that enables one to write "The End." Even with the achieving of many life-goals and the satisfaction brought by many accomplishments, there is always that nagging sense of incompleteness and the deep feeling that one has only begun to learn how to apply much of the wisdom that has finally come only with advancing years of experience. Even at that, we are quite to recognize that none of that wisdom is in any sense complete.

As I have given eulogies for hundreds of people through the years, my question has always been: Would the creator of all good things and the preserver of all that really matters discard this life in a trash heap of things that are no more? Is the crowning achievement of God's creation of so little consequence that a few brief years is the best God can give to lives that were made with such potential? With so much remaining to be achieved, with so much becoming yet to be done, with so many new discoveries yet to be made, and so much territory yet to be explored, will there be no more time and no other place for such possibilities?

I believe that there is. What is wrapped up is our brief earthly journey – our limited time on planet earth. James Weldon Johnson has captured in poetic form (the only way I think you can talk about such matters) in his poem "The Judgment Day":

> And I hear a voice, crying, crying:
> Time shall be no more!
> Time shall be no more!
> Time shall be no more!
> …
> With a wave of his hand God will blot out time,
> And start the wheel of eternity.[156]

In *Living With Death*, Helmut Thielicke provides some weighty theology for reflection on what he calls the Easter *mystery*. By using that word, he is letting us know he is discussing something that cannot be quickly analyzed, "proved," or easily explained. It is beyond our time-horizon and usual methods of comprehension. It is a faith word but that does not mean it isn't true.

> Two things may be seen that very profoundly affect my existence. First, I always take myself with me. I am always my past, for I can never give up my identity. Second, I cannot posit myself afresh and begin anew from the beginning as in cyclical time. My time-line is irreversible. It is directed to its end. It is "soon gone, and we fly away" (Psalm 90:10) The initiation of

---

156 James Weldon Johnson, *God's Trombones* (New York: The Viking Press, 1945), 56.

eternal life by Christ's resurrection gives a new quality to past, present, and future.[157]

ANOTHER TIME AND ANOTHER PLACE

One of the problems I have found with most of the books on this "timeless time" we call eternity is that the writer attempts to provide too much specificity. One of my sermons on the afterlife I titled "A Promise, Not a Blueprint." It is based on John 14:2. The KJV provides the translation with which most of us grew up: *"In my Father's house are many mansions...."* Better and more accurate translations provide a clearer meaning of the text: *"My Father's house has plenty of room."*

Jesus does not provide any details except that it is his Father's house and there is more than adequate space for all. The book of Revelation calls this house the new Jerusalem with gates of pearl and streets of gold. Dimensions are even provided which give the assurance of more than many rooms. To take these descriptions literally is to miss the power of metaphor. What is not metaphorical is the assurance of a place of life in its fullest – no more pain, loss, or death. The promise of a life of relationship and grace to a degree it is impossible to imagine. A good summary is Paul's citing of Isaiah 6:4 in 1 Corinthians 2:9: However, as it is written: *"What no eye has seen, what no ear has heard, and what no human mind has conceived – these things God has prepared for those who love him"*.

No further information is coming. That certainly is enough for me. Whenever I am pressed for further words about the next life, I often say, "Let me put it this way. You will certainly not be disappointed." Or, I ask, "In doing the math of eternity: Do you believe the next life should be indicated with a minus, equals, or plus sign. Is the next life *less* than this one, *equal* to this one, or *more* than this one?" Almost without hesitation, the answer comes, "Oh, a plus sign. What's coming has got to be *more* than this life!"

---

157 Helmut Thielicke, *Living With Death* (Grand Rapids: William B. Eerdman's, 1983), 140, 159.

I agree. Except that plus sign is a plus like nothing we can possibly imagine (1 Corinthians 2:9).

In their zeal and misguided enthusiasm, some have brought ridicule and worse to the concept of heaven and the next life. Lewis Black in his book *Me of Little Faith* cites an example that does not reflect a basic Christian point of view. With his sharp wit he writes:

> Another group that caught the world's attention was a semi-religious one with overtones of alien fantasy called Heaven's Gate. They were my favorite. They were the best. Why? They were homegrown! Nobody grows more nut jobs with the same panache as the good old U.S. of A. To begin with, their leader was Bo and his partner was Peep. Go ahead, look it up – it's in the public record. They were Bo and Peep. And they went around the country holding meetings in order to increase their flock. I don't know about you, but if I was at a meeting and the guy in charge said, "My name is Bo, and this is Peep," that would be the end of the meeting for me. I'd be out of there.[158]

From this "cynic at large" comes an example that bears no resemblance whatsoever to our basic beliefs about the next life. We are not a bunch of "nut jobs" with a Bo-Peep mentality. I don't know that Black has ever been exposed to theology that doesn't require your mind to remain parked at the door. We believe there is more. We believe there is another time and another place with dimensions that defy description. (I wish Black could read a little bit of Thielicke!)

An Easter Faith

The Gospels were written backward. They really begin with the resurrection and move backward to provide the details of what preceded that event that brought the church into being. I have a sermon with the title: "Faith's Equation: Christianity Minus Resurrection Equals Nothing." Following the crucifixion, the disciples

---

158 Lewis Black, *Me of Little Faith* (New York: Riverhead Books, 2008), 119.

take up their former occupations and it appears that the "Jesus movement" has run its course. Nothing accounts for the change that occurs except the resurrection event. The one message that changes everything is, "We have seen the Lord. He is alive!" No myth or propaganda could have resulted in the zeal and commitment that marks the once fearful and in hiding followers of Jesus.

Somewhere I read in a reference I have lost, how one pastor comes into the pulpit on Easter Day: "I arrive as the latest in a long list of runners and I tell my congregation: 'Peter saw him risen… (Pant, pant, pant)…and he told me to tell you.'"

Two concepts have helped me take "Easter Faith" out of the box. "Walter Brueggemann suggests that we consider Easter a verb…That God is in the business of Eastering.…We don't allow our faith to spill over into those places God wants to be an Eastering presence, and where God intends to use you and me as such Eastering presences out there in the world."[159]

The second is that eternal life doesn't start when we die, it starts now. *"I give them eternal life, and they shall never perish; no one will snatch them out of my hand"* (John 10:28). This is only one of the passages where the gift of eternal life is present tense. We have eternal life, beginning now.

What does this kind of assurance do for our daily living? John Wesley was once asked, "If you knew that you would die at twelve o'clock tomorrow night, how would you spend the intervening time?" He responded:

> "Why, just as I intend to spend it. I would preach tonight at Gloucester and again tomorrow morning. After that I would ride to Tewkesbury, preach in the afternoon and meet the society in the evening. I should then repair to friend Martin's house, as he expects me; converse, pray with the family, retire to my room at ten o'clock, commend myself to my Heavenly Father, lie down to sleep and wake up in glory."[160]

159 *Journal for Preachers* (Montreat, NC: Easter, 2016), 18.
160 Loraine Boettner, *Immortality* (Phillipsburg, NJ: Presbyterian and Reformed Publishing Company, 1956), 36.

Two Testimonies

There are many experiences that can be related where people become convinced that their departed loved ones have another existence. The first I give is from an "ordinary" person. The second is from a respected and honored writer and theologian.

> I once asked a woman dying of cancer how she was. "Fine," she said. "My sister just sat on the bed to talk with me for a while." The woman was ninety-two and her mind was very clear; her sister had died over a decade earlier.[161]

Frederick Buechner tells about a very good friend of his who suddenly died in his sleep. This gave no chance for any kind of a goodbye. A couple of months later he and his wife were staying with his widow overnight in Charleston, South Carolina. He had a dream that night about his friend:

> I dreamed that he was standing there in the dark guest room, where my wife and I were asleep, looking very much the way he always did in the navy blue jersey and white slacks that he often wore, and I told him how much we missed him and how glad I was to see him again....Then I said, "Are you really there, Dudley?"....His answer was that he was really there. And then I said, "Can you prove it?" "Of course," he said. Then he plucked a strand of blue wool out of his jersey and tossed it to me, and I caught it between my index finger and my thumb, and the feel of it was so palpable and so real that I woke up.... When I told that dream at breakfast the next morning, I had hardly finished when my wife spoke. She said she had noticed the strand of wool on the carpet when she was getting dressed. She was sure it hadn't been there the night before. I thought I was losing my mind, and I rushed upstairs to see, and there it was – a little tangle of navy blue wool that I have in my wallet as I stand here today.[162]

---

161 Kathleen Fischer, *Imaging Life After Death* (New York: Paulist Press, 2004), 131.

162 William Zinsser, *On Writing Well* (New York: HarperCollins, 1998), 105-106.

THE REAL QUESTION

The dominant theme of Job is the question: Who has the last word? For me, that is *the question*. Others in the book of Job have many words to speak and Job also has a pretty good chunk. God doesn't have anything to say to the group until Chapter 38 and Job only has 42 chapters. God seems to arrive fairly late on the scene but this allows everyone to have their say. Finally, God speaks... and God has the last word.

God has more than the last word. John Ortberg tells of a painting in museum of a chessboard and of a visitor who makes the comment, "The king has one more move." He uses that comment for the title of a chapter in his book *When the Game Is Over It All Goes Back in the Box*. He is confident that death is not the last move but that the King (God) has one more move.[163] I believe that God has the last word and his last word is *life*. He also has the last move on life's chessboard and that move is into a new dimension of existence – into a new time and a new place. It's not over until God speaks his last word and makes his last move.

AFTERTHOUGHT

Even before he could read, my younger son could never get enough of Dr. Seuss. We read countless of his books together. A few years ago, I stumbled across one of his poems about words, language, alphabets...and much more. It is titled *On Beyond Zebra*:

Said Conrad Cornelius o'Donald o'Dell,
My young friend who is learning to spell:
"The A is for Ape. And the B is for Bear.
The C is for Camel. The H is for Hare.
The M is for Mouse. And the R is for Rat.

I know all the twenty-six letters like that...

---

163 John Ortberg, *When the Game is Over It All Goes Back in the Box* (Grand Rapids: Zondervan, 2007), 229f.

So now I know everything anyone knows
From beginning to end. From the start to the close.

Because Z is as far as the alphabet goes…"
Then he almost fell flat on his face on the floor
When I picked up the chalk and drew on letter more!

A letter he never had dreamed of before!
And I said, "You can stop, if you want, with the Z
Because most people stop with the Z.
But not me!

In the places I go there are things that I see
That I never could spell if I stopped at Z.
I'm telling you this 'cause you're one of my friends.
My alphabet starts where your alphabet ends."[164]

The Christian's spiritual alphabet starts where the world's alphabet ends.

PERSONAL REFLECTIONS

In the eighth decade of life, I'm still working on:

- Realizing that I will never get things wrapped-up in this lifetime.
- Allowing the Easter mystery to bring a new quality to my past, present, and future.
- Using Easter as a verb and striving to be an Eastering person.
- Trying to live in such a way that I can give Lewis Black a better example of faith in the next life than Bo and Peep.
- Living with the confidence that God will have the last word and the last move.

---

164 Spencer Burke and Barry Taylor, *A Heretic's Guide to Eternity* (San Francisco: Jossey-Bass, 2006), 146-147.

QUESTIONS FOR REFLECTION AND DISCUSSION

1. What about your life do you feel will always remain unfinished and incomplete?
2. How do you respond to the idea that Jesus gave us a promise and not a blueprint of life hereafter?
3. How do you do the math of the next life? On what basis have you made your decision?
4. What impact does it make on your daily living to believe that eternal life begins now?
5. What do you make of the two testimonies about the sister and Buechner's friend?

Epilogue

But I trust in you, Lord;
I say, "You are my God."
My times are in your hands.... – Psalm 31:14-15a

I'm writing this epilogue in the middle of a year (2016) filled with increasing terrorism both homegrown and ISIS inspired. There is a debate raging (literally) over how to deal with the terrorists and what kind of gun control should become law. I have no words of wisdom to add (I have actually heard very few) but acknowledge that this is the world in which I live and continue to learn.

What I know is that much of the most inspired writing in both the Hebrew and Christian Scriptures comes from times that were chaotic and filled with terrorism of a different kind. Both the nation of Israel and the young Christian church faced some of the worst times they ever experienced. And yet these periods gave us much of our Old and New Testaments. People continued to believe that their times were in God's hands and that living redemptively as his people should continue. And it did.

What I have tried to outline in this book are some of the things I believe I am called to continue to pursue in any place at any time. Some of the emphases may change and additional ones may be called for but the basic list remains unchanged. "The second half of life presents us with the opportunity to develop increased depth, integrity, character – or not."[165] I do not want to be one of the "or nots" because of these difficult times. I only have to casually glance at the biography section of my library to remember all of the people from every walk of life who, in the second half of life, developed increased depth, integrity, and character in spite of overwhelming odds.

One of the books I am now reading is particularly relevant. Thomas Merton's *Faith and Violence* was written at a very troubling time in American history. Violence and unrest in many forms

---

165 Angeles Arrien, *The Second Half of Life*, 5.

plagued our nation; Merton provides insightful and challenging material for his time and for our time. In one of the chapters he discusses the prison meditations of Father Delp who was imprisoned and later executed as a traitor to Nazi Germany in time of war. Merton writes in 1968 about the danger we face in living in such times:

> The dominating factor in the political life of the average Christian today is fear of Communism. But, as Father Delp shows, the domination of fear completely distorts the true perspectives of Christianity and it may well happen that those whose religious activity reduces itself in the long run to a mere negation, will find their faith has lost all content.[166]

The temptation is never far away to live by fear instead of faith (by which I mean trust). The Bible is filled with admonitions to fear not and questions like: *Where is your faith? Why are you afraid?* We, of course, have every good reason to be afraid – if we forget whose we are and view our world through the lenses of unfaith.

Eugene Peterson has always spoken to me both in his books and in his biblical paraphrase, *The Message*. Some of his words form a fitting conclusion to this epilogue:

> Every day I put hope on the line. I don't know one thing about the future. I don't know what the next hour will hold. There may be sickness, personal or world catastrophe. Before this day is over, I may have to deal with death, pain, loss, rejection. I don't know what the future holds for me, for those whom I love, for my nation, for this world. Still, despite my ignorance and surrounded by tinny optimists and cowardly pessimists, I say that God will accomplish his will and cheerfully persist in living in the hope that nothing will separate me from Christ's love.[167]

---

166 Thomas Merton, *Faith and Violence* (Notre Dame: University of Notre Dame Press, 1968), 50.

167 Eugene Peterson, *A Long Obedience in the Same Direction* (Downers Grove, IL: Inter-Varsity Press, 1980), 72.

BIBLIOGRAPHY OF QUOTED SOURCES

Alda, Alan. *Things I Overheard While Talking to Myself.* New York: Random House Trade Paperbacks, 2008.

Arrien, Angeles. *The Second Half of Life.* Boulder: Sounds True, 2005.

Bagby, Daniel. G. *Seeing Through Our Tears.* Minneapolis: Augsburg, 1999.

Bartlett, John. *Familiar Quotations,* 14th Edition. Boston: Little, Brown, and Company, 1968.

Bass, Dorothy. *Receiving the Day.* San Francisco: Jossey-Bass Publishers, 2000.

Bauman, Stephen. *Simple Truths.* Nashville: Abingdon Press, 2006.

Berends, Polly Berrien. *Coming to Life.* San Francisco: Harper and Row, 1990.

Black, Lewis. *Me of Little Faith.* New York: Riverhead Books, 2008.

Boettner, Loraine. *Immortality.* Phillipsburg, NJ: Presbyterian and Reformed Publishing Company, 1956.

Braybrooke, Marcus. *Life Lines.* New York: Thornsons, 2002.

Bridges, William. *Transitions: Making Sense of Life's Changes.* Reading, MA: Addison-Wesley Publishing, 1980.

Brilliant, Ashleigh. *Appreciate Me Now and Avoid the Rush.* Santa Barbara: Woodbridge Press, 1981.

_____. *I Have Abandoned My Search for the Truth, and Am Now Looking for a Good Fantasy.* Santa Barbara: Woodbridge Press Publishing, 1991.

Brokaw, Tom. *The Greatest Generation.* New York: Random House, 1998.

Brown, Michael E. *Bottom Line Beliefs.* Macon: Smyth & Helwys, 2009.

Burke, Spencer and Taylor, Barry. *A Heretic's Guide to Eternity.* San Francisco: Jossey-Bass, 2006.

Butler-Bowen, Tom *50 Psychology Classics.* New York: MJF Books, 2007.

Cannato, Judy. *Radical Amazement.* Notre Dame: Sorin Books, 2006.

Capon, Robert Farrar. *The Mystery of Christ & Why We Don't Get It.* Grand Rapids: Eerdmans, 1993.

Carr, Jimmy and Greeves, Lucy. *Only Joking.* New York: Gothan Gooks, 2006.

Carruth, Gorton and Ehrlich, Eugene. *American Quotations.* New York: Wing Books, 1988.

Carthlegehayes, Mary. *Grace.* New York: Crown Publishers, 2003.

Casey, Michael. *Toward God.* Liguori, MO: Liguori/Triumph, 1996.

Chittister, Joan. *Wisdom Distilled from the Daily.* New York: HarperSanFrancisco, 1990.

Claypool, John. *Stories Jesus Tells: The Parables.* New York: McCracken Press, 1993.

Clemmons, William P. *Discovering the Depths.* Victoria, BC: Tafford Publishing, 2006.

Cloud, Henry. *Never Go Back.* New York: Howard Books, 2014.

Cooper, Burton Z. *Why God.* Louisville: John Knox Press, 1988.

Couglin, Paul. *No More Christian Nice Guy.* Minneapolis: Bethany House, 2005.

Cunningham, Lawrence S. *Thomas Merton: Spiritual Master.* New York: Paulist Press, 1992.

Fischer, Kathleen. *Imaging Life After Death.* New York: Paulist Press, 2004.

Fisher, Len. *Weighing the Soul.* London: Weidenfield & Nicholson, 2004.

Foster, David. *A Renegade's Guide to God.* New York: Faith Works, 2006.

Freeman, Chriswell. *When Life Throws a Curveball, Hit it.* Nashville: Walnut Grove Press, 1994.

Freeman, John. *The Tyranny of E-Mail.* New York: Scribner, 2009.

Friedman, Thomas L. & Mandelbaun, Michael. *That Used to Be Us.* Detroit: Thorndike Press, 2011.

Fulghum, Robert. *All I Really Need to Know I Learned In Kindergarter,* 15th Anniversary Edition. New York: Ballantine Books, 2003.

Garrish, B. A. *The Pilgrim Road.* Louisville: Westminster John Knox Press, 2000.

Gawande, Atul. *Being Mortal.* New York: Metropolitan Books, 2014.

Gladwell, Malcolm. *Blink.* New York: Back Bay Books, 2005.

Greeley, Andrew. *Confessions of a Parish Priest.* New York: Simon & Schuster, 1986.

Gregory, David. *How's Your Faith?* New York: Simon and Schuster, 2015.

Grizzard, Lewis. *Elvis is Dead and I Don't Feel So Good Myself.* Atlanta: Peachtree Publishing, 1984.

Haidt, Jonathan. *The Righteous Mind.* New York: Pantheon Books, 2012.

Henry, Patrick. *The Ironic Christian's Companion.* New York: Riverhead Books, 1999.

Herman, Doug. *What Good is God?* Grand Rapids: Baker Books, 2000.

Higdon, Ronald. *But If Not.* Cleveland, TN: Parson's Porch Books, 2011.

_____. *From Fear to Faith.* Cleveland, TN: Parson's Porch Books, 2011.

_____. *In Changing Times.* Gonzalez, FL: Energion Publications, 2015.

_____. *Surviving a Son's Suicide.* Gonzalez, FL: Energion Publications, 2014.

Hinckley, Gordon B. *Standing for Something.* New York: Three Rivers Press, 2000.

Homiletics Journal.

Hunsinger, Deborah van. *Bearing the Unbearable.* Grand Rapids: William B. Eerdman's, 2015.

Jinkins, Michael. *Letters to New Pastors.* Grand Rapids: William B. Eerdmans, 2006.

Johnson, James Weldon. *God's Trombones.* New York: The Viking Press, 1945.

Jones, Gregory Knox. *Play the Ball Where the Monkey Drops It.* New York: HarperSanFrancisco, 2001.

Journal for Preachers. Montreat, NC: Easter, 2016.

Kalas, J. Ellsworth. *The Pleasure of God.* Louisville: Westminster John Knox, 2016.

Kelly, Matthew. *The Rhythm of Life.* New York: Fireside, 2004.

Kurschwitz, ed., Robert B. *Attentive Patience.* Waco: Baylor University, 2016.

Lamott, Anne. *Grace Eventually.* New York: Riverhead Books, 2007.

_____. *Plan B.* New York: Riverhead Books, 2005.

Lessing, G.E. *The Oxford Dictionary of Quotations,* Third edition. Oxford: Oxford University Press, 1979.

Levoy, Greg. *Callings.* New York: Three Rivers Press, 1997.

Lutz, Frank. *Words That Work.* New York: Hyperion, 2007.

Mathison, John Ed. *Treasures of the Transformed Life.* Nashville: Abingdon Press, 2006.

McHugh, Adam S. *Introverts in the Church.* Downers Grove, IL: IVP Books, 2009.

Merchant, Dan. *Lord, Save Us From Your Followers.* Nashville: Thomas Nelson, 2008.

Merton, Thomas. *Contemplative Prayer.* New York: Image Books 1969.

_____. *Faith and Violence.* Notre Dame: University of Notre Dame Press, 1968.

Meyer, Rabbi Levi. *Ancient Secrets.* New York: Villard Books, 1996.

Meyers, Robin R. *Saving Jesus From the Church.* New York: HarperOne, 2009.

Muller, Wayne. *Sabbath.* New York: Bantam Books, 1999.

Nozick, Robert. *The Examined Life.* New York: Simon and Schuster, 1989.

Oates, Wayne. *The Struggle to be Free.* Philadelphia: Westminster Press, 1983.

O'Malley, William. *God, the Oldest Question.* Chicago: Loyola Press, 2000.

Ortberg, John. *Everybody's Normal Till You Get to Know Them.* Grand Rapids: Zondervan, 2003.

_____. *When the Game is Over It All Goes Back in the Box.* Grand Rapids: Zondervan, 2007.

Peck, Scott M. *Gifts for the Journey.* New York: HarperSanFrancisco, 1995.

Peterson, Eugene. *A Long Obedience in the Same Direction.* Downers Grove, IL: Inter-Varsity Press, 1980.

Poole, Charles. E. *Beyond the Broken Lights.* Macon: Smyth & Helwys, 2000.

_____. *The Flute Beneath the Gold.* Macon: Smyth & Helwys, 2002.

_____. *The Tug of Home.* Macon: Smyth & Helwys, 1997.

Queen, Chuck. *The Good News According to Jesus.* Macon: Smyth & Helwys, 2009.

Rawson, Hugh. *Unwritten Laws.* New York: Castle Books, 1997.

Roberts , Jr., Joseph. *Sideswiped by Eternity.* Louisville: John Knox Press, 2006.

Rohr, Richard. *The Naked Now.* New York: Crossroad Publishing, 2009.

Rohr, Richard and Marton, Joseph. *The Great Themes of Scripture: New Testament.* Cincinnati: St. Anthony Messenger Press, 1988.

Ross, Maggie. *Pillars of Flame.* San Francisco: Harper & Row, 1988.

Shannon, William. H. *Seeking the Face of God.* New York: Crossroad Publishing, 1988.

Simmons, Philip. *Learning to Fall: the Blessings of an Imperfect Life.* New York: Bantam Books, 2002.

Sitz, Bob. *Not Trying Too Hard.* Washington: Alban Institute, 2001.

Smedes, Lewis. *A Pretty Good Person.* New York: Harper and Row, 1990.

_____ *Standing on the Promises.* Nashville: Thomas Nelson Publishers, 1984.

Smith, Huston. *Tales of Wonder.* New York: HarperOne, 2009.

Stella, Tom. *A Faith Worth Believing.* New York: HarperSanFrancisco, 2004.

Sweet, Leonard. *Out of the Question...Into the Mystery.* Colorado Springs: Waterbrook Press, 2004.

Thielicke, Helmut. *Living With Death.* Grand Rapids: William B. Eerdman's, 1983.

Tickle, Phyllis. *The Divine Hours: A Manual for Prayer.* New York: Doubleday, 2000.

Tolle, Eckhart. *The Power of Now.* Novato, CA: New World Library, 2004.

Tuleja, Ted. *Quirky Quotations.* New York: Galahad Books, 1992.

Wall de, Esther. *Seeking God.* Collegeville, MN: The Liturgical Press, 2011.

Ward, Geoffrey C. *American Originals.* New York: HarperCollins, 1991.

Webb, Lance. *Conquering the Seven Deadly Sins.* New York: Abingdon Press, 1995.

Weiner, Eric. *Man Seeks God.* New York: Twelve, 2011.

Wuest, Kenneth. T*he New Testament: An Expanded Translation.* Grand Rapids; William B. Eerdmans Publishing, 1952.

Zacharias, Karen Spears. *Will Jesus Buy Me a Double-Wide: Cause I Need More Room for My Plasma TV.* Grand Rapids: Zondervan, 2010.

Zinsser, William. *On Writing Well.* New York: HarperCollins, 1998.

ALSO FROM **ENERGION PUBLICATIONS**

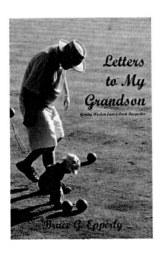

... let the preconscious child within yourself wake up to bite-size surprises of grace for complex issues.

Kent Ira Groff
Retreat leader, spiritual guide
Author of *Honest to God Prayer*
and *Clergy Table Talk*
Denver, Colorado.

ALSO BY **RON HIGDON**

Blending biblical and conventional wisdom with relevant stories and experiences has produced a superb guide toward a healthy ministry and church.

Bill Wilson
Director, The Center for Healthy Churches

MORE FROM ENERGION PUBLICATIONS

Personal Study

Holy Smoke! Unholy Fire	Bob McKibben	$14.99
The Jesus Paradigm	David Alan Black	$17.99
When People Speak for God	Henry Neufeld	$17.99
The Jesus Manifesto	David Moffett-Moore	$9.99

Christian Living

Faith in the Public Square	Robert D. Cornwall	$16.99
Grief: Finding the Candle of Light	Jody Neufeld	$8.99
Crossing the Street	Robert LaRochelle	$16.99
Surviving a Son's Suicide	Ron Higdon	$9.99

Bible Study

Learning and Living Scripture	Lentz/Neufeld	$12.99
Those Footnotes in Your New Testament	Thomas W. Hudgins	$5.99
Luke: A Participatory Study Guide	Geoffrey Lentz	$8.99
Philippians: A Participatory Study Guide	Bruce Epperly	$9.99
Ephesians: A Participatory Study Guide	Robert D. Cornwall	$9.99

Theology

Creation in Scripture	Herold Weiss	$12.99
Creation: the Christian Doctrine	Edward W. H. Vick	$12.99
The Politics of Witness	Allan R. Bevere	$9.99
Ultimate Allegiance	Robert D. Cornwall	$9.99
History and Christian Faith	Edward W. H. Vick	$9.99
The Church Under the Cross	William Powell Tuck	$11.99
The Journey to the Undiscovered Country	William Powell Tuck	$9.99
Eschatology: A Participatory Study Guide	Edward W. H. Vick	$9.99

Ministry

Clergy Table Talk	Kent Ira Groff	$9.99
Out of the Office: A Theology of Ministry	Robert D. Cornwall	$9.99

Generous Quantity Discounts Available
Dealer Inquiries Welcome
Energion Publications — P.O. Box 841
Gonzalez, FL_ 32560
Website: http://energionpubs.com
Phone: (850) 525-3916

CPSIA information can be obtained
at www.ICGtesting.com
Printed in the USA
FFOW02n0829270517
35939FF